Unspoken

Writers on Infertility, Miscarriage, and Stillbirth

Edited by
Whitney Roberts Hill
and Elizabeth Ferris

Unspoken

First published in 2020 by
Life in 10 Minutes Press
Richmond, VA

lifein10minutes.com/press

Distributed by IngramSpark & Life in 10 Minutes Press

ISBN 978-1-949246-04-9
Printed in the United States of America
First Printing, 2020

LIFE IN 10 MINUTES PRESS

Stories that are brave + true.

Also by
Life in 10 Minutes Press

This book is dedicated to all the babies whose spirits dwell among us,
To the brave writers whose stories are recorded here,
And the many more that remain unspoken.

Notes

Versions of some of the essays and poems in this collection have also appeared in other publications. We are grateful to those places for allowing us to share these words here. They are (in order of appearance):

The Wordless: The Unspoken and Unnamed, How to Explain Infertility When an Acquaintance Asks Casually, IVF Egg Retrieval, Reciprocal IVF, My Seven-Year-Old Son Becomes a Christian, and *Early Menopause,* by Allison Blevins, appeared in the author's chapbook *A Season for Speaking* (Seven Kitchens Press, 2019). *How to Explain Infertility When an Acquaintance Asks Casually,* also appeared in Mid-American Review.

Water Baby, by Hanna Bartels, is a modified version of an essay published by The Manifest-Station in May 2017.

I Look for Love in Loss, by G.M. Palmer, was originally published at E-Verse Radio.

A version of *Am I Allowed to be Sad?* by Seema Reza, appeared in Entropy in March 2016.

A version of *We Have Pets,* by Carla Sameth, originally ran in MUTHA Magazine in 2015. It also appears in the author's memoir, *One Day on the Gold Line: A Memoir in Essays* (Black Rose Writing, 2019).

Table of Contents

Foreword

When Life in 10 Minutes Press formed on a spring day in 2018, in the back room of a writing center in Richmond, Virginia, we threw around words and phrases we wanted to associate with the work we would do. We settled on two purposes, two guiding principles. The first was to continue the mission that our writing community had been engaged in for the past five years: to promote stories that were brave and true. The second was the desire to publish the books we wanted to see in the world. Later, in private, this idea of publishing the books we wanted to see would transmute for me into a single word: needful. I wanted us to publish books that were needed.

Unspoken is certainly one of those books. Childbearing loss—a term at once too narrow and hopelessly imprecise—is an achingly widespread experience, and yet public narratives are lacking. Thankfully, there are signs that this is changing. Just last year University of Minnesota Press published *What God Is Honored Here?: Writings on Miscarriage and Infant Loss by and for Native Women and Women of Color.* (We know that in the US, the infant mortality rate for Black and American Indian infants is double that for white infants, and studies suggest that Black women have double the risk of experiencing miscarriage compared to white women.)

I suspect people have always been telling these stories. As long as there have been wounds, there has been a desire to show them to the light. But what happens when these stories only feel safe to tell to oneself in private? Or when, after being told by a doctor that childbearing loss is, as one writer in this collection experienced, "as common as a cold," one finds the book shelves or magazine racks or Facebook feeds strangely silent? What happens when well-meaning but careless family members tell you the time has come to forget and move on?

I don't know if stories heal. Healing is a complicated, imperfect thing. But I do think they help. It is my great hope that whoever you are and whatever your experience, the words on these pages will hold you. That they will offer something to you that you need.

— Elizabeth Ferris

Introduction:
A Word About Language

When I was a child, I loved to stand out by the jetties at Garden City Beach in South Carolina, across the street from my grandmother's house—a towering stucco row-house carved out like a slice of wedding cake and plunked down between the inlet and the ocean.

I would walk along the beach, low, where the sand was packed hard by surf, and notice the edge of washed-up reeds and detritus. The tidemark. Evidence of where the water had been, and would come again. I loved standing at the edge watching the wavelets—sometimes falling short, sometimes surpassing, their predecessors.

During those meditations on the edge of the water, I tried to use my mind to control and predict what the next wave would do. I wanted to be the energy force, to quicken what I knew was coming, to use my mind to pull the water up and over my bare feet.

I felt that same impulse when it came to the language used in this book. I know that the landscape around childbearing loss is changing; those who have experienced it are sharing more than ever before. And many of them are seeking a new vocabulary to describe their experiences, because they have found words like "infertility," "miscarriage," and "stillbirth" patriarchal or insufficient. I wanted this book to be a part of that transition to a new language. To pull on the tide hard, like the moon.

There is no singular word for the parent of a child who has died. There are terms for other such persons marked by loss—orphan, or widow, for example. Bereaved Mother or Bereaved Father; but some of us don't feel like we can lay claim to these monikers. Am I still a bereaved parent if my child never took a breath? What if their heart never had a beat? What if they were only a dream that never materialized at all?

From the moment my first baby died inside me I began searching for the language to describe my experience. The day after I came home from the emergency room, I lay in bed writing out every detail, some of which I later shared, desperate for the life I had harbored to leave a mark on the world. In the months that followed, I went searching for others who had traveled a similar road. I was trying to find a book like this one— a collection of stories companionable with my own.

Friends and family members alike faltered in their attempts to comfort my husband and me. They held their flimsy words up, ill-equipped by our culture to say much more than "sorry for your loss" or "you'll have another baby." Some cast their words aside, unoffered. Those who didn't acknowledge our grief made us feel most isolated of all.

The medical industry has a different set of horrible words for what befell me, and has befallen so many others. "Threatened Miscarriage" my hospital discharge papers read, as though I had stood them all up at gunpoint, crazy-eyed, threatening to drop my forming baby on the cracked linoleum floor. And later, "No Evidence of Pregnancy," as though none of it had ever happened. In the early days of this book, Elizabeth and I were tasked with deciding what to call it, and how we might talk about the breadth of kindred griefs we wanted to collect here. We traded ideas, feeling keenly the clumsiness of the available language, wishing we could invent something better than the words we'd been given to talk about these things.

Miscarriage is threaded with culpability and patriarchy, as if a mother is to blame for failing to carry her baby. Pregnancy loss evokes absent-mindedness. Infertility is not just the lack of an experience or state, but an experience or state of its own, specific, grueling. And stillbirth speaks nothing of the gauntlet of labor or the perfection of rosy-lipped newborns without breath.

But the tide has not turned yet. These are the words with which our culture is most familiar, and so we used them, hoping their familiarity would make these stories easier to find. Asking for forgiveness from the generations to come who will no doubt invent better names.

For now, in order to speak the often unspoken, we use the old words. Our hope is that they send out a beacon to make these stories findable in the deep sea. To let the next mother, father, brother, sister, or grandparent know they have companions on this road. None of us is alone, and we don't have to be silent any longer.

— Whitney Roberts Hill, March 2020

The Wordless: The Unspoken and Unnamed

Allison Blevins

At six months pregnant, the limits of language make me cry
over every sound: all the lowing cellos—sounds strung up

on laundry lines, displayed like underwear flapping itself crisp
and unopening, how the bow moves like wind across strings—

every tinny brass—beaten into my palms, stalled and toed
up my arms. I don't play an instrument, so I'm missing

words to explain how every sound feels, how it feels
to grow another woman inside me, how to explain God
    —mostly that—

and the child with my hair and eyes I'll never someday have. How
can *sadness* mean all this? The words, nameless as the Water-
    Drawers,

the Damsels, the 10 Concubines of David—all the unworded women,
unmouthed and untongued mothers and daughters. Some
    word must

exist to give language to all the women who exist only in the sigh
    and struggle—
the shuffle on of boots in lingering lines—all those lost
    to silence.

Stars Beyond Our Galaxy

Valley Haggard

On my first Shamanic Journey several months ago, stretched out flat on a yoga mat on the floor of a downtown apartment, I traveled to the lower world where I met my sister who'd never been born tending all of the babies I'd never had. I saw them, I spoke to them. Tears streamed down my cheeks. It was so loving and so, so good. There was no feeling of loss in the Lower World. Mere moments had passed since we'd all been together. Life on earth was a flash, a brief intermission. We'd be together again.

It's now been 12 years since I had a miscarriage—or a uterus. Nearly a decade of trying and trying and trying again seems lifetimes gone—and can be brought back in the flash of an ultrasound photo, the thump of a heartbeat, the whiff of a hospital bed. So much blood, so much pain, so much loss. So much hating new mothers and cheerfully pregnant women. So many times my womb turned from a cradle to a grave. Six times. Six babies gone. I named half of them—Ruby, Vera, Cosmo. The others went unnamed, like distant bright memories, like stars beyond our galaxy.

During my decade of fertility, before my hysterectomy, before my uterus was sent to Pathology and all of the fibroid tumors and blood and pain were at last gone for good, I rarely walked on steady ground. I felt closer and further away from God than any other time before or since. We communicated in a constant push pull of *please please please.* Why didn't you let me have those babies? I asked God, and God said, *I did.*

Still, I hated anyone who suggested that all of my losses were meant to be. Now though, looking back from the middle distance

I think *maybe maybe maybe*. I learned something about my capacity for suffering and strength. I gained compassion for an entire world of invisible, unspoken loss. I looked at everyone I saw through a different lens. The lens of *what were the odds that you were born? That you made it all the way from there to here?* Slim to none.

Everyone I saw was a statistical, miraculous anomaly. But, above and beyond all, I was inoculated with the best antidote for child loss there is: a perfect baby. When the doctor suggested my newborn had positional club feet because of my heart-shaped uterus and that he may be more susceptible to chest infections because he was premature, I wanted to punch that doctor in the face. How dare he suggest my child was anything less than a miracle?

When my son was three years old, he blamed himself for the death of his siblings. He'd asked me so many times for a baby brother I'd finally told him that there had been another baby but that the baby had died before she was born. Days later my son came to me, crying, barely able to get the words out. Had he eaten all of the food in my belly? Was that why the other baby died? It was like the time a dish had shattered and he'd told me, lower lip trembling, tears spilling from his aquatic blue eyes, *I was afraid you wouldn't love me anymore.* How can you wipe out a thought like that fast enough? How can you take it away? *Never never never,* you say, and you hold your baby boy, really just a brilliant meteor passing through your orbit, as tight and as long as you can.

Water Baby

Hanna Bartels

It started with red and it ended with water.

In the hospital, after a spot on toilet paper, the doctor asked if I would like to see the ultrasound screen.

No, I said.

She began moving the wand. I watched her face, waiting for some sign of relief, a flicker of assurance. Finally, she said, *I do see a pregnancy*, and I felt hope rising like a balloon in my throat. But I should have known, pregnancy does not mean baby. The power of a word, the unmaking.

I don't see a heartbeat, she said.

She tilted the screen toward me, pointed out my baby. On the screen, suspended in time, it looked so big, so unbroken.

The doctor placed a picture in my lap, proof that for a handful of weeks I was never alone.

I was discharged. There was nothing more she could do.

Baby, fetus, pregnancy, tissue, blood, nothing. The slow progression toward empty.

When my husband came home, we held each other in our entryway. We didn't speak. We watched the Chicago Cubs win Game Six of the World Series and my husband kept his hand on my knee, his fingertips pressed against my skin, anchored to him so I couldn't float away.

Later, while he slept, I slipped into the bathroom. The contractions I'd been told to expect had begun, and I felt primal. The acute ache and spasm, heavy waves and transient quiet, the hemorrhaging. The understanding that I was giving birth to something that resembled nothing at all but that, somehow, I knew I could identify. I thought, for a moment, about waking my husband to hold my hand while I labored. To be there for the birth of nothing.

Finally, a splash, and I knew without looking that the gestational sac, my baby, was sinking to the bottom of the toilet bowl. I plunged my arm into the bowl. I cupped the sac in my hand, let out a sound, a gurgle or a strangled wail, then dropped it back into the depths of the toilet. I sank to the floor, my arm propped against the seat. I wanted to see my baby. I wondered what it would look like. If I could see its little fingers, the cyst that had killed it, its eyelids still fused shut against transparent skin.

For a moment, my baby slept at the bottom of my toilet bowl while I decided if I could stomach flushing it down. I noted the time, 11:58pm, like it was somehow important, although I knew my baby had already been gone for days.

I flushed.

There was a red stain on the porcelain. I would scrub it out the next morning.

That I never knew my baby, its voice or its smell, didn't seem to matter. I felt the void of its absence more absolutely than I ever could have imagined. A phantom limb, perennial and transcendent of all notion of knowing.

I started mentioning my loss in conversation, a knee-jerk reaction to the mention of motherhood. Oh, yes, I was pregnant too, but now I am not.

The silence was cavernous. The sharp intake of breath, the gentle turn of conversation. The quiet discounting of an experience.

Eventually, I compartmentalized this scrap of my identity because it was easier than telling them, the mothers, that for a time, I was part of their club. That I was lucky enough to host a life that briefly touched our world with a rush of euphoria before moving on into eternity.

But then, on a trip to Japan, I learned of *mizuko kuyō*, a service to memorialize babies lost in pregnancy. Mizuko, meaning "water child," a baby that lived for its own infinity in the water of a womb. A word, a ritual for something lost.

And for me, speaking about this unspeakable thing, this story of simultaneous birth and loss, feels like a memorial, the cauterizing of a great wound. Honoring the life that made me a mother, too.

Just one day after my miscarriage, almost to the minute, my husband and I watched the game-winning catch of the World Series, thrusting our Cubs out of a 108-year drought. My husband took my hand. Since the moment our baby's heart stopped beating inside of me, the Cubs had won every game of the series, battling back from a 3-1 game deficit to win the whole thing.

I think our baby likes the Cubs, he said.

The beauty of pregnancy, then, lies in the fact that the mother and the father become party to creation. Cultivating a life, fervently, fiercely loving it as the universe weaves it into being. We created something together. A little infinity in the water that slid out of me that November midnight and left me suddenly alone. And after it was gone, we were still here, holding each other together so we couldn't float away.

Thistle's Story

Jennifer Jurlando

"These tests can be wrong, can't they? I mean, just because it SAYS I'm pregnant, doesn't really mean I absolutely am, right?"

And just like that, before the wedding planning books had even been removed from the bedside table, the pregnancy books moved in. It was January 7th when I took the test. I started spotting a couple of weeks later and went to see my doctor. I sat in the restaurant before my appointment and willed God and my ancestors, the Universe and anyone else who could hear my silent begging, to let the food before me go swiftly to the babe and make her strong.

She was fine. I saw her heartbeat and was reassured that the presence of that little flicker made a miscarriage much less likely. A friend told me to enjoy every moment of the pregnancy.

"Look, if you have a miscarriage and you have worried the whole time, you will only have bad memories of the whole thing. Love every moment you have being pregnant. Then, if anything does go wrong, you'll feel good about the time you had."

As we grew together, I was amazed. I was on the phone with my dad the first time I felt her move. It was not the flutter that I had heard of so often. It was a little, explosive BUMP, and from then on, for many months, she seldom stopped dancing. She loved me to read to her and, hell-bent on creating a little genius, I read all of my favorites along with stories in French and Italian. She moved quietly to the prescribed time with classical music, but DANCED and shook, celebrated and grooved to my favorites. Anything with a banjo made her happy. She loved the Dixie Chicks and my favorite bluesmen.

She played games with her daddy, he tracing his finger across my belly, she following and delivering thumps and love through my skin. Lucky me to be stretched, like physical eavesdropping, to feel the love between them. He talked to her and played the harmonica for her. She abused him when he tried to sleep close to us.

I realized that my mother had felt this movement from me.

We had ultrasound pictures. We had baby showers. We had a much-too-long list of baby names. It was hot and we were in the waiting phase.

Philip was working the midnight shift and I stayed up late at night, sleeping in with him in the morning. I finished *The Awakening*, and she hiccuped in my belly, bouncing the book through the final chapter. The long, drowning swim. I went back to bed.

That evening, we danced in the kitchen to Ray Charles. "I am soooo happy, Philip. Thank you." A big storm was blowing, roads were shutting down and downtown Richmond was washing away. I realized that I hadn't felt her move lately and called some girlfriends. "Does that mean that labor is coming?"

I drank the world's biggest milkshake and lay on my side. Nothing.

I called the doctor, and we left for the hospital. My husband—the state trooper—and I got lost on the way to the hospital that we passed every day.

We arrived and made jokes with the nurse about the weather and my crazy boots. I undressed and she tried the Doppler. Philip sat and held my hand while she summoned the doctor and the ultrasound. The on-call doctor called in another doctor.

The room was dark and we could see her, quiet on the screen. The doctor sat on the foot of my bed and told Philip to stand close to me as he delivered the news that she was no longer alive in my womb. We knew. We had known since shortly after our kitchen dance. We hoped otherwise, but we knew.

I asked for a C-section, unable to fathom the idea of walking around with her still in my body. The doc shuffled his feet and made something up about being without an anesthesiologist. My doctor would be there in the morning and we could talk to her about it.

They would not let us leave. We called our folks. I called my brother, my best man, my best friend. He tried not to cry, because I wasn't, and promised not to leave until the storm had passed. A few hours later he was there with us, listening to the IV make sounds like some foreign instrument, not crying with me and only gently correcting me for making totally inappropriate jokes about the lack of repercussions should I drop the baby.

Later, in the darkness, my husband wrapped around my silent middle, I finally sobbed.

The sun rose the next day.

My doctor arrived and convinced me that a C-section might make future pregnancies harder. The Pitocin started early and my resolve not to have any meds dissolved. No chance now that the epidural would hurt my baby. I felt relieved to have something to DO and set about the business of birthing my daughter.

That evening, well after the shift change, everyone who had cared for us was still there, watching me push. The labor that I had been so afraid of was coming to an end. I was almost finished with my work, with my journey, with my time cradling my daughter below my heart. And then, she was here. One nurse said, "Oh, she is perfect," and I fantasized about escaping a stirrup to kick her in the teeth. My doctor said, with such sorrow, "Oh, baby..." and proceeded to count the number of times the cord was wrapped around her neck. One...Two...Three...Four. "And two true knots."

They wiped her off and then handed her to me and Philip and we cried. Tears rained down from my husband's eyes, mixing with mine on my face and on hers. Everyone left us alone with her. There are things that I remember about her, but mostly now, I remember her weight in my arms. All glorious six pounds, thirteen ounces of her. Vaguely, I can imagine her fingers and long toes, but I am not sure if they really looked like I imagine them now, or if I have since replaced them with the images of her later-born brothers' bodies. We held her for a long time, returning her to the nurses while she still held the heat of my womb. We wouldn't see her again, despite many offers from nurses to bring her back to us. We didn't let anyone else see her. In retrospect, I wish I had taken some pictures. I wish that we had bathed her. I don't waste my time wishing I had noticed her kicks slowing down, or wishing that I knew WHY this was the end of her journey—a hospital room and two weeping and then laughing, devastated and proud parents.

We did not have a service for her. We huddled close and held on tight to each other, shoring up our marriage with a mortar of shared love and joined grief. We named her on her first birthday, eager for her to have a proper place on her soon-to-arrive brother's family tree. Thistle Sidonia.

I imagine we will always be close to each other, my daughter and me, and that we have, somehow, always been together. I am grateful for all that she taught me about loving my children and listening to my heart. She has moved from a place inside my body to a place inextricably wrapped in my soul.

Thistle was born in 2004. For years, my husband felt phantom kicks. We still dance in the kitchen. Ray Charles has not been banned. My three sons talk about their sister. Friends send me pictures of thistles they pass on walks, and each one is a gift. We eat cake on her birthday and tell her brothers, again, all about her.

Other losses have come and have changed my sense of her life. Not a day passes that I don't think of her or know her impact on my life and the lives of others. Losing my daughter changed my sense of the world, my assumptions about life's promises. With years separating me from the day that I held her, she has become integrated into every part of my life. I am her legacy, a sacred gift that I am grateful for in every moment.

Robin

Sarah Artley Luong

Every April I take my classes of freshmen outside to gather sensory input for poems. After being cooped up inside the institutional walls for most of a school year, we are all pretty exhilarated.

I watch them explode into the new air, wrangling and tangling all around. They wallow in the freedom and the chilly freshness of early spring. Most of them cannot help but dance and giggle. Only a few, here and there, walk solitary, contemplative, as I have asked.

It was on one such walk that we witnessed something drop, dark and lifeless, from the clutches of a robin flying straight over our heads.

It dropped swiftly, its descent forming a line perpendicular to hers, landing soundless on cold, hard earth.

We ran to bend and peer at a dead baby bird; its enormous, dark blue eye bulged behind a filmy layer of skin, its tiny old man face and curled toes lay silent.

My students were sad. They held a quiet moment for the baby bird.

Mama had returned to her nest, and she seemed to be watching us, perched on a ledge of the school.

Staring up at her I tried to discern some sense of sadness. Was she feeding the others right now? Or was that the only one left?

Once, I'd had a whole nest of baby birds on my front porch. My wife and I had watched with gleeful anticipation as the eggs cracked and the tiny wet blobs pushed out. But one day we came home and the nest was gone.

It was a different April when I buried another dropped promise, dark and shapeless, in a flowerpot on my doorstep. It had made it to seven weeks, then masqueraded as a life for four more.

The flowerpot brought me no comfort.

Postcards from Heaven

Lyndsey Lang

Hi, Mummy. How are you today? Please know I got here safely.
Our family were quite surprised I came here as a baby.
They told me I should let you know that they'll look after me.
I wish I could have stayed, but life had other plans for me.

Hi, Mummy. I turned one today. I know that made you sad.
I watched you wake up crying for the year we never had.
I hope you read this postcard, and you know my words are true.
You'll never be alone when I am watching over you.

Hi, Mummy. I'm just writing to make sure that you're okay?
I'm four now, and I should be there and starting school today.
I watched you drop my siblings off, and when you were alone,
you thought of me. Your tears they fell, in the car on
    your way home.

Hi, Mum. It's me. My teenage years have finally arrived,
and still the love you have for me inside you hasn't died.
I know you often wonder who I would have grown to be.
Would I be like you? Or dad? Or maybe just, simply, me?

Mum. Can you tell my sister that she made the perfect bride?
We were all here watching full of love and so much pride.
I see I'm now an auntie, too—my brother is a father!
It truly is a gift to see him raising his young daughter.

So, Mum. I've watched you all these years—
    too many years apart.
Now, old and frail, but still I'm here inside your aging heart.
I've waited for a lifetime for us both to be together.
Take my hand, the time has come, for us to share forever.

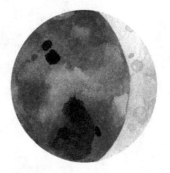

Motherline

Whitney Roberts Hill

She died peacefully in her home on the morning of her ninety-fifth birthday. The day before, my mother had called to ask if I wanted to speak to her, offering to hold the phone up to Marian's ear as she lay unconscious in the back bedroom, the one that smelled of dust, from whose windows you could see the pear tree and the clothesline.

"No," I said.

I planned to be there in two days. A five-hour drive, south and east, from Virginia through the Carolinas. I imagined getting to kiss her papery cheek and telling her I loved her in person. But I never got the chance.

It sounds contradictory to say that my grandmother was never a mother, but for most of my life I thought it was true. She was, technically, my step-grandmother. My father's mother died of cancer when she was not yet a grandmother.

My grandfather and Marian had each lived through a lot of hardship by the time they married. My grandfather lost an arm to a wayward propeller aboard a Naval aircraft carrier during World War II; he watched as his flight instructor was decapitated by the same blade. My grandfather blacked out and woke up in a VA hospital. He was twenty-one.

After the war, there had been housefires, car crashes, the deaths of spouses, parents, and siblings.

In their home the past was sealed from view as solidly as the drywall behind the pine-paneling of their living room. But, they allowed me—ever the snooping, burgeoning writer—to plunder the cabinets for my late grandmother's photo albums and scrapbooks. She kept a diary of their honeymoon, spent visiting relatives. There were photos of her as a dark-haired infant in her own grandmother's arms, her at four, in a flowery bathing cap, her as a toddler, fat-cheeked and clinging to her sister's hand in the garden, her at eighteen, waving from a parade float, her coke-bottle figure fitted into a swimsuit.

Still, my grandfather and Marian (PaPa and MaMa) never talked about themselves. Growing up, the details of the first fifty years of Marian's life remained fuzzy to me; what little information I had came second- or third-hand. I knew that she had taken in a teenage niece and nephew after her sister and brother-in-law both died, and my father's two youngest siblings would have been at home, still in high school, when she married my grandfather. But, to my knowledge, MaMa had never been a mother herself.

My mother called back to say they'd found a handwritten note with final instructions from Marian. In my imagination it was written in blue ink on yellow legal paper (the kind my grandfather favored) and tucked into her jewelry box.

"She told us not to put her birth year in the newspaper," my mother said.

"Can't be lettin' the town gossips know how old you are," I joked.

"Guess not. But, shoot, if I live that long y'all can put it on a billboard."

We laughed.

"There's something else," my mother's voice trembled slightly. "She wants to be buried in Nichols."

"Not with PaPa?"

"No," her voice broke. "She wants to be buried beside her baby."

There had been a baby boy who lived just thirty-six hours.

On the day of her funeral, his headstone was covered in scruffy green carpet, which surrounded the red clay earth where her body would be enfolded. It was bitterly cold, windy, and sunny, the dirt pocked by crabgrass and tree roots. An ostentatious spray of yellow roses hung over the top of her casket.

We huddled close under the tent while the priest said his remaining words of committal:

Rest eternal grant to her, O Lord.

And let light perpetual shine upon her.

My cousin's wife stood beside me holding their youngest child against her chest, a baby boy four months old, wrapped in a heavy blanket against the cold. MaMa had met him, her first great-grand-son, only a few weeks earlier. As they lowered her casket, he let out a cry, quickly carried off by the wind.

*

Preston Elvington Riddick was born at the community hospital on the morning of July 27, 1961 and named after his father, Marian's first husband. At 8:30 the following night, July 28, he succumbed to cardio-respiratory failure from what was then named Hyaline Membrane Disease. It goes by the more practical Infant Respiratory Distress Syndrome now, and it has evolved from a death sentence to something highly treatable, due in part to the fact that it also claimed the life of the president's infant son, Patrick Bouvier Kennedy, just two years after Preston.

In 1961, the common practice for maternity care was twilight sleep. A cocktail of Scopolamine and Morphine, and padded straps holding a woman to her hospital bed. The drugs induced terrifying hallucinations and violent struggle from the laboring mothers, but they retained no conscious memory of the births.

It was routine to keep babies in the nursery, away from mothers. Breastfeeding was considered inferior to formula-feeding, a heathen practice relegated to the poor, and (in the American South especially) to people of color. The mother's body was conceptualized as useless to the baby after birth.

Was he a beautiful baby? I want to ask her. Did she see him alive? Did she hold his body when it was still, feel it growing cool and stiff? What did she do the next day? And the next?

Did they long for him all the years of their marriage before he came? She would have been thirty-nine on the summer day her son was born. There would be no more chances. The grains left in the hourglass were simply not enough.

Every year his birthday and death day had come and gone. Another set of thirty-six hours passing by. I want to know what year she stopped crying. If she ever woke up on that day but didn't remember until after breakfast. Preston would be a man my mother's age, a little step-brother to my father, a rangy fourteen-year-old when his mother remarried my grandfather. A father himself, and perhaps a grandfather, by now.

He is easy to imagine. My grandmother's bright blue eyes, her first husband's deep dimples. Chubby legs squeezed into knee socks and saddle shoes.

I wonder what became of his layette and bassinet. His glass bottles and Marmet Felicity stroller with its whitewashed bicycle wheels, the cedar chest full of diapers and handknit blankets. Did she pack them away, or did someone do it for her?

*

Seven weeks to the day after my own baby died, I entered the sanctuary of St. Stephen's Episcopal Church. A day or two after my miscarriage the thought had come unbidden, *I want to go to church.* Instinct, maybe. A need for conference with the God of my childhood. The One to whom my parents had commended *my* newly-born spirit over a marble baptismal font, my ancestor's lace christening gown flowing through the priest's palm and reaching nearly to the floor. The One to whom I had recommitted myself at twelve, with the Bishop's hand on me, and his words, *Strengthen, O Lord, your servant; empower her for your service; and sustain her all the days of her life.*

Sustain her all the days of her life.

It felt insufferable that my life would march onward into the future without my baby, eclipsing him, carrying no sign that he had ever been.

I sought out a specific service. Not Eucharist Rite II, performed in broad daylight, to pew after pew of wool coats and perfume. No. I came on a rainy, cold night, through a side entrance, to a church with no priest, no lector, no electric lights aside from the red Exit signs. I stopped on the way in and struck a match, lit a votive candle, curtsied to the altar at the edge of the pew in the way I've watched my mother do countless times, before sliding in and down the long plank of cool wood. Candles burned around the pillars of the church and across the altar. The stained-glass window was backlit in the darkness, pouring reds and blues and yellows onto the crowns of our heads. Everyone sat in silence. I unfolded the kneeler, and bowed my head in prayer. The old panic came. *What do I say?* But in the years since I have stopped coming to church, I have learned to talk to God in my own way. I folded the kneeler away and waited.

Lord grant us a peaceful night and a perfect end.

In a mixture of Latin and English a circle of cantors sang to God in polyphonic harmony, their voices tumbling over the pews and sliding their fingers around my neck. By the time they got to the psalms I was crying as silently as possible, not bothering to wipe away the tears in the dark, my eyes trained on the stained glass.

O God, make speed to save us.
O Lord, make haste to help us.

*

Marian's funeral service was held in the Parish Hall of the Episcopal Church of the Advent. Standing-room only. The room was trimmed in dark wood, with a wall of many-paned windows looking out onto an ancient magnolia tree. The priest raved about Marian. What a woman of God she had been, he said, interrupting the service to make personal remarks. This isn't traditionally done in the Episcopal Church. The Rite of Burial leaves no space for eulogizing. It is about death more generally, and mostly about eternal life, indifferent to the past details of the departed.

We were in the Parish Hall because a hurricane the previous fall had damaged the sanctuary. That afternoon, after milling around the reception eating finger-foods and talking to locals, I wandered through the church with my younger cousin. The floor had been ripped up in preparation for its replacement, and the enormous lace-etched glass windows were half-boarded, awaiting new panes. The pews were stripped out, as was the altar rail and the lectern. Still, it was without question, a church.

*

"We should name him," I said to my husband.

He was a him. Have I mentioned that? Immediately I felt such strong masculine energy from the invisible being inside me. A boy to be born in August. A Leo. None of this felt right, exactly. I'd always intuited I'd have a daughter first. And the intermingling of a Sagittarius and a Gemini hardly seemed like a Leo. I would have gotten used to being wrong about these things. I would gladly be wrong about them, and meet my son in the late summer heat. I would give almost anything.

I decided we should name him because I found it hard to say the sentence, "I'm thinking about The Baby." or "I'm missing The Baby." or "I'm sad about The Baby." I needed a shorthand, to help my mouth form around the truth. I needed a quicker way to say, "I know I look like I'm on the shore, but I'm actually drowning again. Right now. In front of your eyes."

For two weeks I tried to think of names. There's something you should know about naming. When I imagined having children, I thought naming might be one of the most difficult parts. Not in the way that sleep deprivation or saving for college or figuring out how to have meaningful conversations with my husband that are constantly interrupted by a toddler, or knowing what to do with my child's bullies or bad grades would be difficult. But, really, naming for a writer? So precious and sacrosanct. The hardest.

"I am thinking about calling him Little Lion," I said to my mother. "That's sweet," she said. "I like it." I was having trouble coming up with a "real name" for him. Both one that I liked enough to choose, and, if I'm being honest, didn't like so much as to waste on a baby whose name would likely never be uttered outside our home. Waste seems like the wrong word, but I don't know what the right word is.

"I keep thinking of an 'A' name," my husband said. This was predictable. Our male cat, who had been my husband's cat before I'd come into the picture, was named Aiden. Which is appropriate for a feisty orange tabby. Aiden is the name of the Celtic sun god, and it means "fiery." He's the only thing my husband has ever named on his own.

Aslan, Ari, Andy-short-for-Leander. These are 'A' names that mean Lion.

He who taught me how to roar. Who woke me up to my animal self, the carnal mother: who splinters furniture into matchsticks, and pounds the floor, and wails and screams and pulls her own hair, and paces on her muscled legs. When I gave birth to him— little shiny red sac that held him—he gave birth to her.

43

On the night of his enlightenment, sitting beneath the Bodhi tree, the Buddha is said to have roared like a lion.

When I was a girl, I had a woven cotton blanket with the image of a Lion laying down with a Lamb. I had a leather-bound Bible, embossed with my name in gold, filled with visions of hell and paradise.

And the lion shall eat straw like the ox.
The nursing child shall play by the cobra's hole,
And the weaned child shall put his hand in the viper's den.
They shall not hurt nor destroy.

Isaiah 11:7–9

*

I find baby Preston's death certificate. It's on a genealogy website, connected to a little box that says "Infant Boy Riddick." I click on it, and a document appears before me. She named him Preston, for his father, and Elvington, for her own family. Baby Preston was also a Leo.

I scroll the names and attending documents. The kindredness I feel with Marian now isn't just with her. I have been inducted into a lesser-known chamber of motherhood by the death of my baby, and among its inhabitants are also my own mother, who lost two babies, and both of my biological grandmothers, who lost one each. A shadow genealogy. A line of invisible mothering.

*

After Marian's funeral, the family returned to my grandparents' house. Cousins gathered around the kitchen table, the sun heavy in the windows. Children ran underfoot, eating from a bunch of purple grapes. My aunt and uncle unloaded the silver from the china cabinet and spread it across the floor; the siblings took turns choosing pieces to keep. "Is there something you want?" my father asked me. "Anything small?"

"Her houseplants," I said, and so he placed them into the back of my car.

At home, I unpacked them, and vacuumed the dirt from the car. Later, after the positive pregnancy test, the blood in the bathroom, after the trip to the ER, I purchased a single stone statue: a Jizo Buddha, guardian of the never-born, as a memorial for Lion. I knit a red hat and bib for the statue, in accordance with the Japanese tradition, and sat him beside MaMa's tumbling pothos plant. Grateful for something to tend, for a life.

3 Poems

Christina Reed

1.
The summer still reminds me
Of being pregnant
And the fall reminds me
Of how I wasn't

2.
Following my miscarriage
I was starved for
Heterosexuality
I had the blood to prove it

I laid in bed waiting for a man
To conceive me
But I couldn't have him
My ribs were showing
And my loins were quenched

I could try my hand at their way
Even for a moment
I could part the vast seas
For a dose of
His sea salt

3.
Adoption after loss means
You
Growing outside of my body
And me
Always knowing you were there

I Look for Love in Loss

G.M. Palmer

When my daughter died,
I could have
frozen up inside;
it was a close shave.

Instead I was saved
by my daughters
who went on living; braved
by their laughter

I am living after
the loss of love.
Now that the broken raft her
body was proves

her spirit has moved
to the life that's best,
it's the memories grooved
inside of me I miss:

how her perfect fist
fit in my hand,
the happy face I kissed
while I was her dad.

Distant Grief

R. Todd Henrichs

The end of our first pregnancy started with just two words, "I'm bleeding."

Her voice was soft but carried an undertone of panic, the kind reserved for moments of true terror. Outside the trailer, night hadn't quite taken hold. Inside, I stood in the kitchen, just on the other side of the wall from where she was, and chalked it all up to a post-coital response. It wasn't until she said those words again, tears heavy in her voice, that I knew it was something more.

"Something's wrong," she said as I peered into the room. She held out a wad of toilet paper. Several bright red dots vandalized its whiteness.

I was 19. She was 18. We'd been married for just over 6 months. We weren't even out of the second month of pregnancy. Miscarriages weren't something that was supposed to happen to us. We were too happy; our faith was too strong; we had done everything right. And yet, there I stood, in the doorway of the two-bedroom tin can we called home, four hours from any family, watching my wife shatter into pieces as her dream of motherhood dripped into the water.

I could tell you that I was there for my wife when she lay in that bed and they told her that she had miscarried. I wasn't.

I could tell you that I was the perfect husband, taking care of her in this difficult time. I wasn't.

I could tell you that I cried with my wife when they brought her back into the room after they performed the DNC. I didn't.

The truth is, there's a reason I don't normally tell my side of the story when it comes to our miscarriage: It didn't happen to me. Yes, the child she carried was ours. But it wasn't a part of me. For her, it was... something greater. I don't even know if I could put it into words. For that matter, I'm not sure I should even try.

Here's what I can tell you. My side. The part that doesn't paint the greatest picture, but it's mine. I made the phone calls. To her mom, my mom, to the hospital (like they both told us to do). I did my best to keep my wife calm when I put her into our car and drove 45 minutes across town from Mayport to the Navy hospital at NAS Jacksonville. I held her hand and talked to her. I don't remember about what, but I must have, because I'm sure she would tell me I was a bigger jerk if I hadn't. When her mom showed up, I stepped back into the shadows so that mother and daughter could share a moment.

I watched as my wife lay in that hospital bed, tears flowing from fear and loss, and tried to be of some comfort to her. But, how could I comfort a woman through a loss I didn't comprehend? This child wasn't a part of me, I wasn't carrying it, I wasn't the one who had to go through the invasive procedure to remove the remnants of lost life.

For me, life kept going. Or rather, it went back to the way it was before we were pregnant. For her, the next two months were anything but what they had been. There were times when she would break into tears, and I would ask, "What's wrong?" out of habit, and immediately regret my existence.

There were times when I would want to be close to her, but she couldn't and I didn't understand and we would argue. There were times she wanted to pack up and head home to her mother and father because she felt she'd made a horrible mistake in marrying a man who just didn't understand what she was going through.

And then there were the two times I got it right. One night, about two months after, I had gone out and found this giant stuffed bunny rabbit. It was brown and white with a blue vest and was every bit of four-foot-tall (without the ears). I surprised her with it, and for some reason that is beyond me, to her that rabbit was the greatest thing. I'd give you a list of possible explanations, but the truth is, she's the only one who knows why it was so special.

And the other time... the other time was about three months later, around midnight, our room was dark and I held her to me in the near silence. She talked about our lost child. She wondered whether it was a boy or a girl. What they would have looked like. If they would have had red hair like her, or freckles like me. She talked for the better part of an hour, and when she had said just about everything she needed to say, she bent her head up toward me, her voice slipped into a soft whisper, the breath of her words on my neck, and said, "What about you?"

I tilted my chin to her forehead, pulled my arm around her a bit tighter, and said, "His name is Gregory."

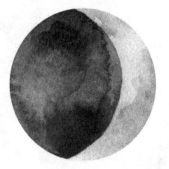

Am I Allowed To Be Sad?

Seema Reza

One evening in Washington, at a dinner celebrating a mutual friend, an acquaintance passed his phone diagonally across the table to me. I declined reading the article in the restaurant, and he agreed to email me the link instead. When I got home that evening, I read the piece, in which Iraqi-born author Sinan Antoon argues that the surge of published writing by veterans, in particular Iraq War veteran Brian Turner's *Here, Bullet,* focuses on the suffering of American veterans who voluntarily enlisted to serve in the US military while erasing the experiences of Iraqi and Afghani civilians caught in the crossfire. On the surface it didn't have a great deal to do with my work facilitating writing groups in psychiatric treatment programs within military hospitals, which ostensibly prompted this poet—a man I barely know—to suspend his cellphone over my dinner. The implication, I suppose, was that by using poetry to help American veterans ease their own suffering, I was contributing to the problems Antoon outlines. I emailed the phone-wielding poet a response inviting a discourse. That I received no reply is only mildly surprising.

The effort to relieve or acknowledge suffering in one place does not deny its existence in another. There is enough suffering to go around. To suffer is to bear something, to be under something. The Wicked Witch of the East suffered from a house falling on her. Then someone took her shoes and her feet shriveled in their striped stockings. But think of the trials of the shoe thief, the poor lost little girl who fell with her house out of the sky. The Munchkins were suffering too, under the tyrannical rule of the witch—that must have been terrible. And the Tin Man, no heart. And the Lion no courage. And the Scarecrow no brain. What's the worst?

In most of my writing groups there is someone who believes their own suffering is the worst. There is always someone who believes their own suffering is unworthy of mention. Everyone has been asked by someone in their lives: *Why can't you just get over it? Why are you choosing to be so miserable?*

The compulsion to compare and measure and (in)validate suffering, particularly the perceived inverse relationship between choice and suffering fascinates me. What factors go into such an equation of suffering?

$$\frac{[((5x+3y)-4z)]/2d \cdot [(9m\,(v+2tw) + c(2g))]/4s\sqrt{f}}{a} = \text{Suffering Worthy of Compassion}$$

Where x is the number of times you felt fear in your home as a child and y is the number of times you braved violence to go to school and z is the number of adults who loved you unconditionally and m is incidents of sexual violence over the course of your life and v is the frequency with which you experienced prejudice and t is regret and w is the people you loved or were responsible for who died and c is the loss of a child and d is a near death experience in adulthood not related to war and g is financial ruin or loss of employment due to circumstances outside of your control and s is acceptance by a peer group and t is the experience of hunger and f is having a safe place to go. And a is personal choice.

And I haven't yet factored in the specific pain of:

Intimate partner abuse
Illness
Disability

Heartbreak
Substance abuse
Homelessness

Or the relief of:

Access to beauty in nature
Good looks
Talent
Travel
Community
Laughter
Meaning
Touch

I don't know how to account for predispositions toward anxiety, sensitivities, social awkwardness, the confines and pressures and advantages of birth order, expensive tastes, below average intelligence, extreme intelligence, a tendency toward insomnia or nightmares.

What sets my own suffering apart is that it's happening to me. What makes your suffering seem worse is that I can't imagine what *that's* like.

Poor You and Poor Me. The diarchy of the kingdom of suffering. The Royal We.

*

My cousin is eight months into a high-risk pregnancy, her first. She is craving French fries and we go to McDonald's. We have gas in the car and dollars in our wallets. It is a beautiful night, all the windows are down. The sunroof is open. In the parking lot she tells me she feels guilty for being sad. "There's nothing to be sad about. I am so grateful to God. But it's overwhelming, this sadness. It comes from nowhere. Hormones maybe." She is bothered, more than anything, by the ingratitude suggested by her bouts of sadness. Everyone is bending over backwards to care for her. How dare she be sad? We are taught to keep our feelings under control, to keep our woundedness cloaked.

When inevitably we can no longer sustain our stoic exteriors, we feel both the grief and an overwhelming sense of shame about feeling it.

Two months ago, she visited my apartment and started bleeding. My sons, their lungs and hands and organs fully formed, these people who left the darkness of my body cloaked in blood, shine like evidence of my good luck. An embarrassment of riches. I herd them into my bedroom, the furthest corner of the apartment. Reward them for their proximity to disaster with weeknight video game time. She is in the bathroom moaning. Her mother on the outside of the door talking her through it. Her husband pacing. Her brother and I are staring at one another wide-eyed. We search the Internet for possible causes. The bleeding subsides, the baby is moving. The bleeding starts again. At three o'clock in the morning, we call an ambulance.

I go to the hospital the next day. She is fine, the baby is fine. The risk is still high, but the crisis has been averted. She says, "I'm so sorry, Seema. Weren't you six months along when you lost your baby? This must have been so hard."

Needle through epidermis, through womb, under soft budding clavicle bone, stilling a tiny beating heart. I chose certain death for him over an uncertain life for all of us. It has been eleven years since I terminated that pregnancy. Each year on the anniversary, I think, *He would have been this many years old.* This year I think: *Eleven, eleven, eleven.*

*

When my son Sam was eleven, he got a leather jacket that made him feel grown up. That year, for the first time, wearing that ridiculous jacket, he pulled his arm from mine as we walked to the grocery store. The natural cleaving. Inevitable.

*

Shame holds people hostage through silence. It fuels the voice that rings in all of our heads that says, no matter what we accomplish or who loves us, "If they really knew you..."

The fear isn't unreasonable. We live in a permanent record world. There is a taboo against changing minds or negating previously held beliefs, against making mistakes. The accusation of "flip-flopping" leveled in political campaigns, the deep digging into the personal histories of public figures—this makes apologies, admissions of mistakes, and the reevaluation of beliefs, absolutely terrifying—a last resort. I say, "I lost a baby." As though I misplaced him by accident. As though he wandered off.

She said, he said, he said, he said, he said, they said, he said, she said, "Seema, you don't understand. I have killed people." Sometimes they say, "There were kids." There is a pause, wide eyes on me. I nod. I think, *So have I.*

There was almost a baby. I would have been his mother. It's not equal. This suffering is voluntary.

In the Middle

Linda Laino

In the middle of my life, in the middle of my marriage, I lost a baby in the middle of my pregnancy. The baby was a girl. I had named her Ruby, after an eccentric great aunt that I adored as a child, much to the chagrin of some family members. My aunt was an unconventional renegade in my traditional Catholic family. A red-headed, red-lipsticked, Camel-non-filter-smoking thorn in the side for some of them. When I was a child, she represented the bold and daring way I hoped to live out my own adult life. I wanted to transfer these qualities to my baby girl through some kind of name osmosis. My choice seemed fitting; "bold and daring" was how I felt about raising a child again so late in life.

When we got married, neither my husband nor I thought we'd have any children at all. Both of us were artists and precariously employed, and life was challenging enough already. A brush-with-death car accident when I was 30 gave us both a dose of mortality. I was shocked that amidst the terror and trauma of my mangled body, the first question my husband asked the doctor was could I still have a child. In that moment, the doorway of possibility had opened. Five years later, we walked through it with our son.

By the time I was 42, I had a seven-year-old, curious, and active boy. Already an "older" mom when I had him, I never considered another child, especially given our lifestyle and financial status. While the wake-up call of the accident explained part of our desire to create a family, I never expected to revisit that desire. But on a trip away from home, I was caught off-guard by my waning biological clock. It's all the insanity I can claim.

That year I went alone to central Mexico to visit my mother-in-law, who lived there with her new husband. I wandered for days through the streets of their soulful, colorful town, falling in love with the children there. All those dark, pleading eyes and sugary smiles seduced my heart, breaking down whatever sensible barriers I had created to expanding our family. One day I simply allowed the feeling. And then it became planted. While still in Mexico, I called my husband and told him, "I want another child." He thought I was joking. By that time, it was a tacit agreement we wouldn't be having any more. But I insisted. I was as sure about it as I was about the fierce love for my son. After I returned and finally convinced him, I was surprised to find myself, in my forties, pregnant within two months. I was elated, and to my delight, so was he.

That is the last time I remember being happy in our marriage.

Following a cautious protocol, we kept our news under wraps. Privately, I reveled in my secret bump, once again tracking all the bodily changes. I absolutely loved being pregnant. Watching my body grow and feeling that first flutter of life felt like a singular privilege. I'd had the most perfect and powerful birth with my son and midwife at the hospital, and I aimed to up the ante this time by having Ruby at home.

I was almost five months pregnant when I came home late one night to find my husband ushering our son out to a friend's house for the evening. It seemed odd. The mood was tense, and there was clear anguish on his face. He said he had received a phone call.

Ruby had tested positive for Down's Syndrome.

Not for the first time I realized how true it is that life can change in an instant. For days, I was in denial. *She was healthy, I was sure of it. There was a mistake in the test. I had seen her sprightly, bubble image. I could feel her move with a jubilant life force. She was perfect!* Only she wasn't. She was one in one hundred chances. It was as if our lives had been handed a new country to discover, only to have that country invaded and destroyed by some malevolent force.

I felt betrayed by my body.

After a long night of shaken disbelief, I woke the next morning with my hand curled around my swollen belly before my conscious mind recognized I would soon be losing that small comfort. My husband felt helpless in the face of our news, and I avoided him, suddenly feeling the burden was mine alone. My body, my baby, my loss. My dive inward festered into a descent that appeared bottomless.

It was August. The heat was unbearable. I had let the weeds take over the garden. Anger propelled me to spend the day severing each intruder at the root. A thousand new fears flooded my veins as I pulled and cut until my hands bled, my anger buried in a mountain of dandelions and crabgrass, soon made lifeless by my own hand.

My husband and I knew all the health complications that could arise. How could we ever bear the financial cost, let alone the emotional one? My feet felt planted into the good-earth life I already had. It seemed insurmountable to begin to fathom such a shift in our course. How could I be loyal to the life I had created and wanted with my husband and son, and also to the life inside that I had created and wanted? My husband and I had previously agreed on the path that was right for us, but we never dreamed we'd get that phone call. With broken hearts, we decided to terminate.

That cruel day ended many things for me: my marriage as I knew it, a sibling for my son, and, for a long while, my ability to function. We would spend the next year consumed with trying to make another baby (to no avail), and more years imagining the road not taken.

To have chosen to create a life, and then be tasked with the decision to end it, was a pivotal path. I will never know if I would have been able to walk the divergent one with the grit and grace required of such a gift. How bittersweet a powerful yet fleeting experience can be. Like crabgrass rooting deep in a garden, it wraps around and informs your life long after it passes.

It's seventeen years later and whenever I think I have finally forgiven myself, I see a teenage girl with Down's, and I avert my eyes.

Please Don't Call Her Stillborn

Lyndsey Lang

I see you've had a stillbirth, the doctor said to me.
She looked up from my notes and smiled, as if I would agree.
"I think perhaps you've read that wrong," I carefully replied,
"I had a little baby girl and, yes, my baby died."
But your daughter, she was stillborn, yes? the doctor asked again.
"My daughter was much more than that. Please call her by her name."
I'm sorry, she corrected, *It's just the terms we use.*
I looked at her and gave a smile but said I was confused.
"Please don't call her stillborn. And let me tell you why.
For nine short months she lived in me. She *lived*. She *was* alive.
She came on family holidays. She kicked inside my tummy.
I loved her from the moment I found out I was her mummy.
She had ten little fingers, she had ten little toes.
She had a head of dark brown hair and a cute little button nose.
She has a little bedroom. I know she'll never use it.
But it's painted in mint green and grey—her brother helped us
    choose it.
You see, she's not a 'stillbirth.' She's family. Our girl.
To you she's a statistic, but to us she is the world."
The doctor, she sat quietly, not knowing what to say.
But then her simple gesture showed I'd changed her mind that day.
She pulled my notes back open and slowly read the words,
And then she looked up with a smile and started to converse.
I see you had a daughter. Let's see, what was her name?

Ah, Evalyn. That's pretty. How old was she again?
Today she taught a lesson and please know that she was heard.
Evalyn was your daughter. And 'stillbirth's' just a word.

Still A Mama

Lisa Sharrock

All I've ever wanted in life was to be a mum. Having experienced infertility, miscarriage, and stillbirth, maybe I should have been more specific in asking the universe to allow me to be a mother to a baby that is alive.

I am a mum, just not in a way that I had ever imagined.

Imagine someone saying to you, "In a couple of hours, everything you know and think about life will be gone. Your whole belief system and soul will be ripped out of you, yet you will remain." You'd say they were crazy, but this is exactly what occurs with the loss of a baby.

Baby loss is multifaceted, complex, and messy. There are no words for the pain. The moment I heard those words "there is no heartbeat," I left my body. Nothing seemed real.

Life philosophies and all parenting approaches fly out the window when a baby dies. (Yes, babies die—but people don't want to talk about it.) Your entire being is deconstructed in ways you never knew were possible. It is unimaginable that anyone can survive the aftermath of baby loss; living on without your child is doing the unthinkable, and continuing to function, is doing the impossible.

Welcome to the world of baby loss—it's not a club we ever wish to join. Interestingly, though, I've found this club is also an amazing place to be. When you meet another Loss Mum, you don't even need to speak. Instantly, you connect with an unspoken understanding. You fight and build resilience over time, and you do survive because the others who endured this before you, they survived.

They are living proof that life goes on past this catastrophic blow to our spirits, and our lives.

In baby loss, we accept, we adjust, but we never get over it.

Just because your baby isn't here doesn't mean that you are not a mum—you are still a mama and you will continue to parent your child every day, just not in the way you had hoped, or planned.

I am and always will be still a mama to Gracie Rose, stillborn on 7 July 2016, and always still loved.

Losing Gracie meant everything I thought I knew had changed, but even in the extreme pain of loss, the decaying of everything I thought I knew is quite liberating. There is strength in being vulnerable. It takes bravery to be open to the hurt; to let it matter. This remarkable loss is the most agony I've ever felt, yet it holds the most love I've ever known. It also has been a new definition of self, an alteration of being, a new way of seeing and a new love— one so strong that it made saying hello and goodbye in the same day worth all the pain.

What I have learned along the way:

- Just breathing is ENOUGH.

- Do not let your suffering become a measuring stick of your love. Oh, how I punished myself in those early days. Relief from your grief is allowed; punishing yourself isn't helpful.

- Your mental health is a priority, self-care is a priority, your existence is a priority.

- You can still be a kind person with a good heart and say no. Do not expect yourself to be the person you were before; this is the new you. You will be getting to know yourself for the next few years. On that note, do not give yourself timescales, particularly in the early months, regarding when you think you'll feel better. I did this and set myself up for the biggest fall of my life.

- You will lose some of your support network. This is normal in baby loss. People will do things that hurt—it is okay to take a year out and re-assess relationships and friendships. It is okay to distance yourself from people who are pregnant and to unfollow people on social media. You are not a bad person for doing this.

- It is essential that you speak with another Loss Mum, it confirms that your thoughts that feel crazy are normal in baby loss. You will share many similar experiences in how society deals with this tragedy.

- Motherhood seems like some cruel joke taunted in your face. There are reminders everywhere. Protect yourself as much as you need to. Be aware that grief stings and stings when you least expect it. Do not fight it. It will always win.

- Your relationship with your partner will be tested. On top of everything else, my marriage ended—my husband decided he didn't want children in his future. Sometimes you just have to accept things with as much grace as you can by choosing love over fear in any situation.

- Live each day to honour your baby. They are never more than a thought away. You will learn a new love that can only be experienced to be understood.

- Live minute by minute if needed, hour by hour, if so, and day by day when you can.

What to Expect When You're Expecting a Miscarriage

Erin Pushman

1. A heartbeat, but none is there. The doctor holding the ultrasound wand pauses. You feel the pause and know something is wrong.

2. Waiting, but not the nine months you'd settled in for. You are waiting for blood, for your body to accept what the doctor has told you.

3. There is no baby. But your flat-bellied womb holds onto whatever was inside. You dress in your non-maternity clothes and avoid mirrors. When you leave the house, you try not to go anywhere there may be pregnant women or babies.

4. Pregnant women and babies are everywhere. You never realized how many places pregnant women and babies go.

5. Cramps, not contractions. OBGYNs have two sets of words: Contractions and delivery; Cramping and passing. Your cramps hurt. You don't want to think about your cervix or what it is doing.

6. A not-baby. You are having a not-baby.

7. Flowers. You go to the Lowe's Home and Garden section to pick out a potted bluebell. There are no pregnant women or babies in the Lowe's Home and Garden section.

8. Silence. No one talks about miscarriage, except online. But you want contact. You want the feeling of someone's hands.

9. Intermittent and discreet pain. In the concrete aisles of the Lawn and Garden section, you fold your body in on itself. But you keep hold of the bluebell.

10. A funeral. But there will not be one. What is there to mourn?

11. The life you were already dreaming for the child that will not be. You were going to have a child, even if you'd told almost no one because the pregnancy was still too early. You were going to dress the child in plaid pajamas; you were going to read the child Beatrix Potter stories; you were going to show the child each new bulb as it pushed through the earth and teach her the names when the buds emerged: daffodils, hyacinths, bluebells.

12. A girl. You were expecting a girl. From the moment you peed on the stick, even before you saw the plus sign and showed it— half-trembling—to your husband.

13. A toilet bowl. Because that's where you pass the pregnancy. You should have known not to stay in the bathroom, but you did not know where else to go.

14. Water, colder than you think it will be. You scoop out the darkest mass of tissue with your hands, lay it on the paper towels folded on the bathroom floor.

15. Life as usual, which goes on around you and assumes you will go with it (because almost no one knew you had been expecting).

16. A shovel. You need a long handle and a broad blade to break up the soil. The hole you dig is wide and deep enough to hold the bluebell's root ball and the baby you wanted and the stained paper towels, too.

17. Tears, which keep coming. If you take an extra-long shower, you can get out most of the day's crying in there, where you can press your hands into your empty belly, and you can't feel the difference between tears and hot water.

18. Confusing periods. Of time, of womb. Your body has its own language and grieves in its own way—more bleeding, longer cycles. You accept all this as recognition of the loss, which must at some point settle, the way losses do.

19. The rest of your life, which does go on, however changed by the baby under the bluebell.

20. A pink candle burning in a votive holder. Two handfuls of years later, your church holds a pregnancy and infant loss service. The number of women there surprises you—all women, no men, except the pastor. All women you know. Women who are older than you by decades and women who are younger than you by decades. Women who, like you, have living children, and women who do not. Women with whom you have not discussed lost babies, until now, when the discussion is a movement, first forward, one by one, to light the candles—pink for girls, blue for boys, white for unknown; then together carrying the candles from the chapel to the courtyard, where you place them on a marble wall above the columbarium; then in a slow exchanging of embrace, of putting empty hands together, all the while standing in the votive candlelight, surprised by its brightness.

Unable to Speak

Dana Arlien

We sat across the desk from the doctor. I felt a strange emptiness open inside me. It was difficult to hear his words across the distance between us, which felt as vast as a chasm, stretching out over miles of open air. I could see his lips moving, the wind whipping the sound away.

The doctor said that all the embryos had arrested. I thought, *Were those my children?* They didn't feel like my children. It felt like a project for the science fair when I was a kid. A project that didn't work. I was as perplexed then as now. Wondering why the potatoes I had carefully planted in fertilized soil, and moistened with water, and placed in a box in a dark cupboard, hadn't burst forth, sprouting long, hungry white shoots seeking the light.

The doctor had stopped talking. I only noticed because his lips were not moving. He seemed to be waiting for an answer to something.

My mouth opened slightly, but I found I could not speak. No sound came.

I looked at my husband, barely registering his face as he watched me. I lifted my hand, although it felt like someone else's hand. It descended slowly to his thigh. I could not look at the doctor.

My husband said, "We are going to take a break." I think that's what he said. But I don't really remember. We stood to leave. My husband asked, "What are the chances on our own?"

"Seven percent," the doctor said. I suspect it was probably zero, but giving a number was a way of giving hope. It was a parting gift.

He could have said it is 93 percent likely that you won't have children. But he didn't.

There had been other strange moments in this journey that feel distorted, like I watched them through a fun-house mirror. Everything seemed unreal. There was my first day back at work after the embryo transfer, when I knew that IVF had failed because I started bleeding. I am a doctor, specializing in Child and Adolescent Psychiatry, and I work in a psychiatric hospital. When I walked into the nurse's station everyone was excitedly talking about the new baby. The baby my colleague had given birth to the very same day. I did not look at the pictures. The nurse asked me, "Don't you like babies?"

There was the moment after "harvest day," as I preferred to call it. As I was coming out of conscious sedation, I said, "I can deadlift 210 pounds." But I couldn't anymore. I'd lost my athleticism during the long process of my body being invaded by medications and hormones and the finest of medical science. Yet another disappointment.

There were all the times that, learning about my infertility, someone told me their conception stories, always unbidden and unwanted. "Just get drunk...there was this time in this hotel..."

I know how babies are made.

The unending vaginal ultrasounds. I had begun to feel like I was an attraction at an amusement park, and I wanted to charge admission.

The doctor said there is always hope. You just do the next thing. And there are many next things. And I wondered if I really deserved to be a mother if I wasn't willing to keep sacrificing myself, my body, for the next thing and the next thing and the next?

My body betrayed me, failed me in this most basic way. And I live with the irony of spending my youth trying to prevent an accidental pregnancy when, it turns out, that was an unnecessary worry. Because we never had children.

The Trauma of Miscarriage

Arden Cartrette

From the moment we pulled into the parking lot, I could feel that things were getting worse. The pain was more intense and the sensation was all too familiar, probably because I had experienced my first miscarriage only four months prior.

As I walked through the double doors into the emergency room, I felt a wave of relief. *Maybe someone in this building could help me.* I needed someone to tell me what was going on with my body.

Three days before, we had learned that our second pregnancy had come to an end, and it was time to induce the physical process of miscarriage. I took four pills and waited for what I thought was my Rainbow Baby to leave my body. After all we had been through, I couldn't believe that we were in this place again.

That night, three nights before this emergency room visit, I thought I miscarried. The pain was the same as the first time around, though that time the miscarriage had been natural. I thought that I had made it through the worst of it, and now I just wanted to heal emotionally and grieve our losses. Days passed and the bleeding was light, but I was still in pain. But on the third day, the bleeding started to get heavier and heavier until I realized that something wasn't right. "I shouldn't be bleeding this much," I said to my husband. I asked him to drive me to the hospital.

At the hospital, I laid in a room that looked like the set of *Grey's Anatomy.* Except I wasn't in a TV show, and this was really happening to me. A nurse asked me to sit in a wheelchair and she took me for a vaginal ultrasound to find out what exactly was causing the excessive bleeding, and what could be done about it. In the radiology room, I began to undress for the ultrasound. Within seconds, there was blood all over the floor.

I sat on the exam table in tears. I was in so much pain, and blood was dripping all over me; I couldn't help but feel embarrassed. When the technician came in the room and saw the blood, her first words were, "Sweetie, are you okay?" She grabbed towels to clean up the blood and helped me remove the blood from my clothes and my legs. It occurred to me in this moment that she hadn't been made aware of how severe the bleeding was. Before this ultrasound, no one had seen the blood. They just asked me to tell them about it.

What was happening to me was unfair and not normal.

Three hours later, I was still losing a lot of blood. I was finally given heavy pain medication and we waited for the on-call OBGYN to come and talk with us about our options. Since walking into the emergency room, I'd needed to replace my maxi pads two to three times an hour. To this day, I remember what it felt like as tissue abruptly left my body. No one could have prepared me for what that would feel like.

As we hit the sixth hour in the hospital, we were finally told that a dilation and curettage (D&C) was our only option because of my blood loss. After the procedure, we headed home to emotionally heal.

The truth is, the trauma that I experienced that day, and the night of my first miscarriage just four months prior, has never left me. At times, because of it, I feel lonely and broken. I can still conjure the physical feeling of losing those pregnancies. Following my second miscarriage, I sought therapy, acupuncture, medication, and meditation to try and handle the PTSD. All I can say is that it does get easier. However, I wish I never had to worry about it.

Not many people are aware of what miscarriage is really like until they go through it.

April

Sarah Artley Luong

Warning: Happy Ending

I knew a baby wouldn't solve the marriage. I knew I wasn't ready to leave. I knew I had always wanted to have a baby. I knew I was 37 when we started. I knew that it had taken seven attempts with Intrauterine Insemination for my wife, and I was sure that mine would take less; I was younger, healthier, and certainly luckier and more deserving.

I learned that I knew nothing.

I didn't know that pregnancies could just slip away without as much as a kick in the womb, leaving me living in a lie, telling friends and making plans. I didn't know that before 12 weeks the medical world doesn't even give you the courtesy of calling it a miscarriage, but a pregnancy loss, because it's less, right? *Is it?* And of course, I did not know how god-awfully common it is. The doctors love to say that. It's so common. Like a cold. Like I should be able to just get over it because so many other people have experienced the same thing.

The first one was my fourth try. I remember the sudden disillusionment I experienced with my body, my good luck. I had always been healthy in all other respects, but I would come to realize that maybe I hadn't had any accidental pregnancies after slip-ups for a reason. That maybe all my years of being gifted with the luck of "good genes" had one small caveat.

The second "pregnancy loss" I discovered on April 1st. I had finally made it to the first Ob/Gyn appointment. The ultrasound revealed a 7-week fetus with no heartbeat on a day that should have been at the end of the first trimester. I dropped the F-bomb in the doctor's office. She recovered nicely. It was the first time we had met, and she had the job of telling me that in fact I was not pregnant, that I likely hadn't been for four weeks, since maybe just the day after the joyful discovery at the fertility doctor. And of course, that this was "very common." I drove straight to my mother's house, 100 miles away, stopping only to get gas. I still remember clearly how impossible it was to work the same card reader at the gas tank that I had worked countless times before. As I drove away with my tank open, a nice stranger tried to tell me. I just glared at her. How dare she try to help me?

I thought everyone else I knew got pregnant by accident. And I hated them. I thought my partner had taken my turn at pregnancy. And I hated her. I thought I could get past it if I had to. We had one wonderful sweet child, and she was indeed my daughter. But I was so attached to the idea of carrying a child. When people told me that the pregnancy itself wasn't that important, I hated them. They were saying that from the other side of it. While I had always been open to adoption, it wasn't something my partner and I could agree on. I felt cheated, resentful, and stuck.

Eight months later I found myself going through yet another miscarriage while driving to Indiana to spend a week with my grandmother. I didn't tell her. She was in the beginning stages of dementia. We looked at the same pictures over and over again. I reminded her of the names of her loved ones again and again, while my insides churned. She mourned the loss of her memories while I let go of yet another possible future. By then, I think I was finally starting to grow numb, or perhaps find some small bit of acceptance. I measured my pain against my grandmother's, and she won. I was starting to understand some of the things that I had never known about this journey. But, what I didn't know was that this would be my last miscarriage.

We continued trying every month or two for another year.

My partner and I discussed moving on to more invasive measures. She was willing to try, but I was not so sure. I had undergone 13 IUI attempts, almost twice the number that she had endured to have our daughter. Where was my luck? My good health? My just desserts? We agreed to try one more IUI and then either quit or move on to IVF.

The timing fell in the middle of a camping trip, so I left our campsite an hour west of town to drive to the doctor's office on a Saturday. By the afternoon I had returned and my then-wife and my daughter and I were all in a rowboat on Bear Creek Lake. I dropped my oar and, without thinking at all, jumped in after it. Getting back into the boat was a lot more complicated than it should have been, and I was sure I had done damage to the delicate situation currently taking place in my ovaries.

Now I have the goofy belief that it was magic water. Or maybe it was the new injections I was taking? Two weeks later came the positive pregnancy test, and soon we would discover that my crazy high hormone numbers were because that life starting in my belly was, unbelievably, twins.

There were many scares, but eventually all three of us made it to 7 weeks, 8 weeks, 10, and finally, finally I began to breathe, just a little. And oh, was I sick. Double sick. Immeasurably, gratefully sick.

Our sweet little first daughter made the announcement at my 40th birthday party. She was four years old, standing on a chair in a pizza restaurant, and so proud to be a big sister.

They were born in April.

Loss Calendar

Hanna Bartels

I had already lost four pregnancies when my physician recommended in vitro fertilization.

Maybe your body can't discern an unhealthy pregnancy from a healthy one, she said.

Even my uterus was desperate to be pregnant.

My husband and I were so hopeful—joyful, even. Every shot, every pill was one step closer to parenthood. I delighted when my bank called to determine if the three thousand dollar pharmacy purchase I had just made was legitimate. I was thrilled to see the bruises blooming on my skin, to fall asleep with a heating pad pressed to my hip, to feel bloated and emotionally drained. To carry a doctor's note and a canvas bag full of needles through airport security.

I'm trying IVF! I told the agent who patted me down.

We took pictures every day, my husband behind me with a three-inch needle, both of us smiling.

My physician retrieved nineteen eggs. *Nineteen!* I checked my phone every hour for the next five days, waiting to hear how many blastocysts survived mitosis. In the end, seven were tested for viability and four were deemed healthy. All girls. I bought the first pink onesie I encountered, held it to my chest when my husband came home.

All girls, I told him. *We are having girls.*

Then, the first frozen embryo transfer. On Christmas Eve, I had my blood drawn. On Christmas Eve, we learned the transfer didn't work. On Christmas Eve, we held each other on our couch.

Our presents for each other: board books about the Chicago Cubs, a *World's Best Daddy* coffee mug, a beautiful pink baby blanket. We were so sure we would spend our Christmas celebrating. My uterus had led me to believe it wanted to carry a child. Our embryos were healthy. Success was all we could imagine.

More tests, more shots, acupuncture, massage, essential oils, desperation.

Our fertility insurance had run out so we wrote a check.

Our second embryo transfer worked. We were anxious, but optimistic. And then, after Valentine's Day, I started bleeding, again. Another miscarriage. Our perfect little girl, our second embryo, slipped out of me the way four of my pregnancies already had.

More tests, more shots, more acupuncture, therapy, jealousy, rage.

We drained our savings account.

Our third embryo transfer: another success. I saw a rainbow from my doorstep, a good omen. And a few days after my birthday, at the first ultrasound, there was nothing. A blighted ovum. The physician stepped out of the room to give us a moment to grieve alone, and my husband held me, my feet still in stirrups, the room still dark.

I was pulled over on the drive home, my eyes so clouded by tears that I couldn't see the road. The police officer escorted me home, asked again and again if I would be okay.

My physician told me I would likely never carry my own child. *I'm sorry to say,* she said.

She suggested surrogacy.

In an act of defiance, we tried again, without IVF. Again, a pregnancy, and again, a loss. This time on the Fourth of July.

Our fourth and final embryo is frozen in time in a row of freestanding tanks at a storage facility in an unknown city. Every year, we get a bill in the mail to keep our baby girl cryopreserved, and every year, we pay it. We added this last embryo to our will: directions for how to handle it if one or both of us should die before she has a chance to implant in a uterus, mine, or someone else's.

Maybe, someday, we will finally meet her.

And now, not a holiday goes by where I'm not reminded of the babies I loved and lost. Our losses have become a calendar. This is the day I learned of their existence, this is the day I said goodbye, this is the day I didn't leave my bed, this is the day I would have met them, held them in my arms, if only. Recurring events that I have never recorded, but always recognize.

Still, I wonder who they would have been. Still, I think of how desperately we loved them, and how we always will.

If only, if only.

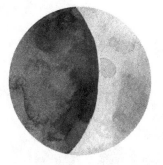

How to Explain Infertility When an Acquaintance Asks Casually

Allison Blevins

After Joan Mitchell's Low Water, *1969*

Think about what is green in green,
how words like silver and bright
sing off every stinging tight space.
I eat. I sit. I repeat. All must have
order. Line up the shoes. Organize
the bottles.
        Remember how some women
drive their cars off cliffs into ravining water,
children asleep, full and snug and shining
in the trunk? These women, on these days,
gold and glittering, must rejoice in flight; air rushes
their lungs, a chorus of women and falling and clattering
metal sings all together. Water cascades and rises,
foretells all the women and children dead,
a history of female drowning.
                Those are not
your women.
        Think of the green in green,
the color that rests just beyond your fingers,
inside, like dirt trapped under grass, like garlic
sprouting, like a long dead bone turned to rock,

tumbled through pulsing years, its ridges and bumps
pressing your flesh, all the small plunges.

                                                 Water cascades
and rises, foretells all women and children.
Spatter and spray cling but eventually disappear.
How terrible it is
                      to release something from your body.

IVF Egg Retrieval

Allison Blevins

Later, we will imagine the children, latchkey, weeping
into a dish that sustains them. Some will die. We are all
pro-choice, the doctor, the nurse, my wife. It is never discussed.
How else to watch what wants to divide? How else
to take the want from my wife's body? Later, we will ask
if we ought to mourn the lost. We imagine them like fish, flushed
or buried by our children, the two already born, next to our
side yard sapling, marked with brown-tipped roses from the bush
by the garage. This is the dead we've buried together. Later,
my wife will swear a lot. Anesthesia. The nurse is an ex-Marine.
My wife, Army. Everyone will laugh. Later, in the hotel,
she will lay her body naked against my back. Our room,
across from the hotel pool, filled with the screams of children.
How else to wait and mourn? Her skin damp, the slow
press and grind of her pelvis against the soft of my legs.

Reciprocal IVF or How to Explain the Similarities Between Ecstasy and Loss

Allison Blevins

These months, I think God might be woman un-named—
creation unclassified by words. I cannot explain loving
this child
      —she is not mine—
                or losing what cannot be lost.
I cannot explain how infertility feels in all my small and deep
spaces. I'm not the only mother to carry loss, lament arrival,
mourn acquisition. Like water swirled to mud, like all the gray
evenings remembering orange. I can't explain this sadness
to my wife,
      —carrying what isn't mine—
                even to myself.
Not even color or sound can explain. No refrain can
   breathe *oohs*
into the roundness, thick and opaque, nothing can
   soften the pitch
and frenzy of my motion,
      —she moves inside me—
                of my ecstasy and loss.
A man in line at a movie theater once told me you can't love
both God and living—human history is one of incompatibility,
   the Fall

means we are always beetles struggling on our backs.
How wondrous it must be to live for death.

                                        —how beautiful—
I cannot explain how it feels to take depths into my body,
to become—held by her hands soft from never having said
    I'm sorry—
to spin without breaking, to give every word to the world,
to swell and swell and swell and stitch it all together at Her feet.

The Phantom of Infertility

Katherine Meyersohn

The surge of grief travels from my stomach to the center of my heart, welling up in my throat, filling my eyes with tears that threaten to spill onto the menu that has been placed in front of me. I clench my jaw and stare at the unreadable words before me, willing myself not to cry in public. Again.

Those four little words: "Do you have children?" make it difficult to breathe. A reasonable question, really, for a waiter to ask, especially on today of all days: Mother's Day. But reason does nothing to quell the lightning charge of emotion—the despair and grief of infertility.

My "no," comes out in a whisper as my husband reaches for my hand, and I look away, trying not to embarrass him and myself, yet again, with a public scene. It amazes me how those words have the power to undo me in a matter of seconds. Still.

Mother's Day: The most dreaded day of the year for women in the midst of the highs and lows of infertility. It's impossible to ignore the continual bombardment of angelic children, offering handmade cards and giant bouquets of flowers to their picture-perfect mothers, that has been spewing across the T.V. screen for the past month. A continual reminder of 'the glass half empty.' I feel bitter and raw, and I hate myself for feeling this way.

I see babies everywhere I turn. My heart surges with love and the desire to be a mother, for who can resist the sweet innocence of a baby? Quickly followed by the hopeless dread and unfairness of what I want so much but don't have. The heart-wrenching dance of infertility.

What do I do with these feelings? The energy it takes to hold myself together is getting overwhelming. I feel like I spend half my day repressing some socially inappropriate expression of my grief and sorrow, and the other half attempting to avoid the triggers for it. It's exhausting, and painful, and my usual supports just aren't working.

Most of my friends and family, try as they may, don't understand. Pregnancy and building a family have come easy for them. It was never a question of "if," it was only a question of "when?" and maybe, "how many?" Their attempts to comfort or help me usually end up falling short. I appreciate their intentions, but I take no solace in their advice.

Still others shower me with unsolicited "guidance"—insisting that my husband and I just need to "relax," "be patient," "reduce our stress," "pray," "get a dog," and/or "adopt." The invalidating, minimizing, and, in some cases, insulting nature of these suggestions only serves to increase my anxiety and resurrect the Inner Smartass in me. I want to fall on my knees at their sanctimonious feet, thanking them for their truly novel suggestions and pledging to name this miracle child (that will now surely materialize) after them in gratitude for such sage advice! My Inner Smartass saves me in moments like these from publicly humiliating myself by doing what I really want to do: burst into tears of frustration and crumple into a sobbing heap of rubble on the floor.

Most people who have never experienced the grief of infertility aren't aware of the enormous amount of energy that is required to function in a world that is terrified of grief and loss and whose social mores demand that the grieving conceal their true emotions for fear of being labeled "bitter," "histrionic," or worse, "unstable" and therefore "unfit" to mother. Not only are women grieving infertility expected to carry this armor of self-enforced optimism at all times, we are shamed for allowing even the slightest hint of the pain and sadness that lurks in the shadows of our smiling faces to escape from behind this culturally-imposed façade, and God forbid, expose others to the grief of our infertility.

The trouble with advising a person who is anxious to relax and be optimistic, especially in the face of multiple disappointments and losses, is that it tends to elicit the exact opposite response. Rather than quelling my anxiety, these overused clichés and throw-away quips send me into a merciless mind-loop of every incident of past optimism that has resulted in bone-crushing disappointment. Serving only to reinforce my worst fears with bona-fide evidence and further expanding the hole in the center of my heart.

I worry that this heartbreak will never end, that there is no way through this pain, no way I will ever come to accept my fate if I cannot have a biological child, and that this grief will change me into an empty, bitter, jaded shell of a person. I want so much to believe that there is something waiting for me on the other side of this grief but, the Phantom of Infertility cruelly whispers, "What if there's not?"

Why Won't You Mention It?

Meredith Hill

Here I am bobbing in this sea of noise
wishing someone would see me.
Acknowledging my loss is all they'd have to do to free me.

Instead, I field questions
about work
and dinner plans
and holiday schedules
and New Year's resolutions
and Netflix series
and travel plans
and Christmas gifts
and family dynamics
and cooking techniques
and new restaurants.

I want to scream, knowing the attention I'd get:
You know I had a miscarriage,
Why won't you mention it?!
Are all of these things really more important to you
than addressing the pain and heartbreak your friend
    has just been through?

I know it's hard when you don't know what to say
and much easier to address the distractions of December,
but for me, right now, this moment of my life is all
    I can remember.

We Have Pets

Carla Sameth

"Why are we stopping here?" my son Raphael demanded as we pulled into the all-too-familiar HMO hospital parking lot and walked in and downstairs to the lab.

My son was five years old, and I had begun looking into having another baby on my own through a sperm donor.

The most beautiful, scary, hopeful, almost orgasmic words I've ever heard are still "you're pregnant," which is what I'd heard a few days before this trip to the hospital. But I'd learned enough to know that early pregnancy was driven by numbers—in my case, levels of human chorionic gonadotropin (hCG)—and the numbers need to be going up fast, at least doubling every couple of days. That was true for a strong pregnancy—and my numbers were low to start with.

There are degrees of being pregnant and not pregnant. Sometimes you don't know for sure if you've lost the pregnancy in the early days. And there are all sorts of terms that mask the despair of a miscarriage: "blighted ovum…" "spontaneous abortion…"

The next morning, after I'd dropped my son at school, I returned to the lab to learn my hCG results. *Was I still pregnant?* The baby, if there was one, would likely have close to the same birthday as Raphael, another Aquarius: creative, already a dreamy intellectual. The numbers were lower. "You should discuss this with your doctor," the nurse said.

I left, sobbing.

As I drove through the Hollywood traffic toward the freeway, my doctor called me. "Carla, do you understand what this means? That you're having a...." He spoke to me like he wanted to slap me to get my attention; I interrupted, heaving sobs.

"Yes, I know," I said. I slowed almost to a stop, and, for a second, I let my head rest on the steering wheel. I hit the windshield wipers on as if they might wipe the tears from my eyes and clear my vision. The doctor continued to talk. It was unlikely that I was anything but miscarrying. He did not tell me to go home and rest, only, "It's so early. There shouldn't be much blood."

After I gave birth to Raphael—my seventh pregnancy following multiple miscarriages—Dr. Beer, the famous reproductive immunologist I'd sought out at the advice of a family friend, said I should try to get pregnant again within the first 18 months. But within a year, my husband and I had separated.

Dr. Beer had often seemed like a mad scientist, with his weird, frequently painful and expensive treatments. Our HMO doctors had only shook their heads; their motto seemed to be, "just keep trying and you might get lucky." Still, there were many "Dr. Beer" babies. And my son, Raphael, was one of them.

Now, five years after Raphael's birth, I couldn't really give myself over to the idea of going through it all again. I knew I didn't have the financial resources. When Raphael was born, a benevolent family member paid off the house-size debt. Now I was on my own, a single mom.

When I was trying to have my first child, I had trouble understanding people who became obsessed with having a second baby. I believed one baby would be enough—manna from Heaven. But then it wasn't. And even if I couldn't have the three children I once wanted, I began to hunger for a second. I felt I could handle two. I had left the nonprofit world for a better paying career track and I had more or less figured out how I'd manage. I never got any rest anyway, so why would it be any different with two; I was willing to kiss any sleep, relationships, and writing career goodbye for another 18 years or so. If I had to choose, I was choosing a second child. The rest could come later.

By the time I arrived home, I had stopped crying. I decided to call Dr. Beer. I hoped that he would tell me something miraculous, that I wouldn't have to start over with the blood transfusions, the new medications.

I telephoned his office, and his nurse arranged for a conference call later that day. On the phone, Dr. Beer told me sternly I should have been in touch with him before I got pregnant.

He instructed me to take another pregnancy test right away, just in case I was pregnant with twins and one had died, causing a temporary dip in numbers. He also told me to immediately arrange for the costly IVIG treatment (Intravenous Immunoglobulin) I'd had with my previous pregnancy.

I felt sick in the pit in my stomach—it seemed ridiculous to spend thousands of dollars trying to preserve a lost pregnancy. I knew my HMO doctors would think Dr. Beer's "possible twins and still pregnant with one" theory was nuts. Still I followed his directions and called my HMO requesting the pregnancy test. Then I flew out of my house to pick up my son.

Raphael was a concrete, living, breathing, sweet body curled up next to me at night.

The next day I didn't rush to the lab as Dr. Beer had instructed me; I didn't call the home health service and order the IVIG treatment. Instead, I went on Raphael's school field trip, as planned. Raphael wore a stuffed animal snake around his neck; the students were instructed to bring a stuffed animal or a picture of a pet on the field trip to the zoo.

"We have pets," Raphael told his classmates, not to be outdone by their boasts of dogs, cats, birds. "We have ants, termites, a bird and her babies," he said, referring to the one of our loud San Raphael birds who had built her nest in the hibiscus tree in the middle of our cluttered patio. I considered her skillful, a bohemian twig artist.

"We also have fleas and skunks," Raphael said.

That day I told myself that if I could continue my life, my very precious life with my living son wearing the blue-green Converse tennis shoes and stuffed snake, I would be okay.

Late that afternoon, I got another blood test. My HMO doctor had ordered it, though he clearly thought Dr. Beer was wacky. He knew there was no baby; it was another miscarriage.

I called for the test results the next day. "The number is down to 16," the nurse said.

Now I had eight pregnancies under my belt—two abortions, five miscarriages, one live birth. Raphael. My miracle son.

"Sometimes adults get scared when life is dark?" Raphael asked me one night at bedtime, soon after my last miscarriage. We were cuddling after his bath and book, the Jewish lullaby tape with songs from around the world playing. He didn't like to sleep alone, in the dark.

I made him repeat his question; it was too deep for me. That was my five-year-old son, the one who insisted on sleeping next to me because his feet got cold. But I was the one who clung to him at night that week after I lost the last pregnancy. I didn't want to use his need to mop up my sorrow. But he always ended up next to me, spooning close.

"That's true," I answered my son. "I'm not afraid of the dark anymore but sometimes..." I trailed off.

I wanted to show bravery, not just tell him how alone an adult can feel. "Sometimes you feel a little scared, but then you get tough," I said.

In the wee hours of the morning, when I awoke, things felt the most stark. Raphael spooned against me made me reluctant to move. But his gentle kicks got me up.

In reality, I felt relief that I was still functioning not even a week after the fallen hCG number told me I wasn't going to have this baby. I was just relieved that I hadn't crawled under my covers for good.

Responding to Raphael's needs pointed me in the direction of the resilience I had carried with me most of my life. I fed, bathed, played with, and cared for Raphael, even while getting hit with heavy cramps the first days of the miscarriage. I still had hot flashes from all the hormones I was taking. Carrying around a thick cloud of defeat, I put one foot in front of the other.

Not long afterward, I made an appointment with a therapist specializing in single parents, infertility, and adoption decisions. I knew enough about adoption to know that it was not as simple as going to the store and picking up a baby, the way some threw it out flippantly, "Just adopt!" It could be months, and sometimes years, of court hearings and waiting, and, in the event of a private adoption, tens of thousands of dollars—to say nothing of the potential loss of an adoption falling through. But unlike my attempts to carry another baby, with adoption, I felt, if you persisted, you *did* end up with a child.

Denial had run its course. I knew that I couldn't risk going through more miscarriages, thrashing myself physically, emotionally, and financially the way I did the first time around before I had Raphael. Early one morning, I wrote Raphael a letter that stayed in my journal, apologizing for my shortcomings as a mother, explaining what I was doing during that time in his life:

I want to tell you that when you were almost five-and-a-half, I decided to try to have another baby. You were always asking me about a brother or sister, and I always wanted more. I used to want three when I envisioned a family that included two parents...and "real" pets like the other kids.

I apologized for not having the energy to read to him every night, for sometimes falling asleep mid-sentence, for not always learning his tap routines to practice with him before his dance performances. And for not picking him up at school every day early at the "goodbye song" when the stay-at-home moms arrived.

Raphael woke up and asked for oatmeal; I put my pen down.

Years later, I wrote a story imagining my own death. In it Raphael was a writer living in Brazil. He had to come back and to go through all my piles of papers, snippets of writing he couldn't read, he wasn't sure he wanted to read. I wondered if he would ever see that letter I wrote, shortly after I had that last miscarriage.

So much had seemed possible during that little window of time: I was pregnant with a potential second child, I had made an offer on a bigger house in the neighborhood, work was growing with two new potential contracts. If I had to pick between these events in my life: baby, new house, and growing business, it was the baby that would win—hands down—even though one might argue the other two would help to support that dream of an expanded family. The first to go was the baby, then the house and possible clients. Everything lost its shine—at least for the first months following the miscarriage.

That summer we went out and bought a leopard gecko. Raphael named him Michael Jordan and fed him crickets. Flowers sprung up outside. Raphael said, "God provided them." At the end of the week, he accidentally smashed the roses with strong bursts of water from the hose. I was sad, but I believed that, in time, the roses would grow back.

My Seven-Year-Old Son Becomes a Christian

Allison Blevins

I tried to explain impermanence, to convince him the Earth is round. Some things you should just know. How motion unsettles the heart like a drum beat off course from the crowd clapping. How familiarity with a scene—a cluster of branches, garbage tumbling along the carved and tarred lines of a drainage ditch, every drugstore—makes you feel home.

On days I'm drowning in déjà vu, I think of every lover who has forgotten the topography of my belly. If I ever tell my son I've found God, this would be both lie and truth, as lovers often lie about memories. Everything unsaid in my body waits just below the skin like the child I can't now have. I am a mother, words tucked behind my teeth. I am a suitcase packed to bursting. On weary days, what is unsaid may ooze out from my uncaulked edges where seeping has been known to happen. I want him to leave what is heavy.

Today, the rains have finally stopped and all the tall grasses are swaying as if cradling a squalling bundle to sleep—both the *shush* and the small mouth bawling move silently together. The part of me that was born wants him to accept impermanence, his nightmares about the mother who left him that follow me from his room, all the warm fears on my cheeks, all I can't control that has led him to this soothing and driftless sleep.

Early Menopause

Allison Blevins

All birds forget how to fly. Crows and blackbirds
walk through parks and cul-de-sacs on invisible stilts.

All schools chain their doors. Women and girls pray wordlessly
in supermarkets between plastic forks and bottled water.

All breezes stop whistling through the stray hairs
on teenagers' necks. Wind purses lips and blows and blows.

All is silent as a man in a black bowler hat. I watch my children
play at the park. My son shoots a stranger's son with his finger.

A girl drags a small stuffed dog behind her on a leash.
The shot hits his temple. The bang is metal piercing flesh,

a pin striking the casing of a round; the noise
bounces off the spiral slide, picnic tables, grills

enshrined in concrete. I can't explain why the skin folding
between my legs is tight like a scar, why men now brush

against me in crowds as if I am a shudder. I can't explain
how it feels in the bowels, on the teeth, on the still smooth bits

of skin in the pit of my elbow—this is where it stings
and hums when you suddenly disappear.

How I Got My "Miracle"

Christina Reed

My wife and I pursued fertility treatments for four grueling years. It nearly killed us. It tore up our marriage, put walls up between us and our friends, and forced us into a period of depression.

We decided to take a chance, fostering a baby that was already a ward of the state. It took two and a half years after being certified to even get the call, but when we did, we were elated. We brought home a beautiful two-week-old baby boy, and we gave him a name. He was incredibly fussy due to an opioid addiction he was recovering from. He didn't sleep unless he was held, his body shook from the withdrawal, and he had an aggressive cry that we could not relieve. He clung to us as if he knew something we didn't.

It didn't take long to fall madly in love.

Then, the bomb hit, one month after he came home with us, he instantly became less ours. His caseworker met with us to explain that there was a family member willing to adopt; the agency finds family placement to be in the best interest of the child. Soon, he would be removed from our care. We knew that in the foster care system reunification with the biological family is always the primary goal. I couldn't be mad at anyone but myself; I signed up for this knowing there was a chance this could happen. And I hated myself for even thinking I could handle it.

We were devastated and more than heartbroken. We stopped leaving the house. We cried over his body as if he was dying; when we weren't crying, we were mostly silent. I couldn't see myself handing over this baby I had taken care of, lost countless nights of sleep over, and thanked God for. My wife and I were the first people to ever love him, and our families already deemed him ours. I hated myself for understanding why him being with a biological family member was fair and right, and, in the long run, may be best. How could this be happening after years of fertility struggles? *Isn't God the least bit merciful?* I wondered. I couldn't understand how genetics could be stronger than the bond that we had established with him.

Two days after we heard the devastating news, my aunt texted me a *Prayer to Saint Jude*. "Say this prayer every day, and you will get your miracle," she told me. I rolled my eyes and didn't respond. I found no consolation in her suggestion. I'd attended Catholic schools for most of my educational career, so I knew enough about Saint Jude to know my aunt meant well. Saint Jude is the patron saint of desperate situations and lost causes; he was one of Jesus's apostles, and possibly a relative of Jesus. I had always been a good Catholic—until I came to terms with being a lesbian. I lost a lot of faith in the church and in God. I knew that what the church taught and who I was, intrinsically, weren't compatible. When I accepted my sexuality, I also accepted I wasn't allowed to pray to Catholic saints, attend weekly masses, or even wear a crucifix. I wasn't obedient enough to be Catholic anymore, I kept telling myself.

I knew I didn't have anything to lose, but still the questions nagged: *Why would God listen to me now? A lesbian who left the church, of all people?* I thought. *Do I even deserve this baby?* I felt so unworthy of him, and like a criminal for trying to take him away from his biological family. My job as his foster parent was to reunify him with his family; I couldn't possibly pray for him to be mine. The problem was, he already felt like he belonged to me. He looked at me like I was his. This small child made me feel worthy of him.

My insecurities felt highlighted. Knowing he was leaving us made everything difficult: his feedings when he looked at us happily, his doctor's appointments when we found out how healthy he was getting, the gifts people were sending, the outpouring of love we were experiencing. I watched my mom bond with him, and I couldn't bear the thought of her losing the only grandchild she'd ever had. Nearly everything made us want to cry.

At this point, I would do anything to feel a connection with a higher power. I needed someone or something to save me from the heartbreak of the situation. My wife and I prayed together, out loud, twice a day, while holding our foster son. I wondered if this was Saint Jude's first time hearing from a lesbian. It felt desperate, and like I was always trying to catch my breath. There was a lump in my throat that made it difficult to speak, but we repeated the words over-and-over. It was all we could do, it was the only power we had over the situation.

After a month of praying, the family member fell through. We were officially matched with our foster son and would soon be adopting him as there was no biological family left to consider. We said the prayer in times of despair, even after we knew the family member had fallen through; we kept saying it till his adoption day on December 5, 2019. We even said the prayer on the way to the courthouse, the day of his custody hearing. It felt like our warrior chant.

I promised Saint Jude a monetary gift to his hospital on the day we were assigned an adoption date. I also promised I would share this story, and encourage people to pray in times of deep despair. I'm not an overly religious person, but I believe this was a miracle.

My wife and I are moms to the most beautiful human. People tell me he looks like me, that he moves his mouth like me, that he's bonded to me. Prayer is powerful, and I am forever grateful to Saint Jude.

Expectant Realities

Angela Haigler

We had arrived in our separate cars. I drove my trusty candy apple red Honda Accord sports coupe. I'd had such excitement when I bought it "pre-owned" ten years earlier. Now, my left knee had started hurting from stepping on the clutch. I'd need something more sensible soon. Jake drove a silver Nissan, his company car. We would grab lunch together, then head back to work after the appointment. We held hands as we walked toward the building and took the elevator to the third floor as directed on the C.A.R.E. postcard. Jake looked cool as always, wearing his new prescription shades and the swagger that made me fall for him a year earlier. 5'9" to my 5'5", we were equals. I loved this man.

My breaths were short and excited, shallow. I tried to remember my meditative practices: breathe in, one-two, breathe out, one-two-three. Maybe here within these walls, seated among these expectant faces, I would be able to complete my entrée into normal life. Never married before, God had blessed me with a husband at 50. And now through a miracle of medicine, perhaps I would be able to experience pregnancy and biological motherhood, too.

The C.A.R.E. staff greeted us with smiles and the assortment of cookies typically found at meet-and-greets and receptions: chocolate chip, oatmeal, and peanut butter. They were good, amazingly good. I grabbed a second one, then a third. None of this was on my plant-based diet. Coffee, iced tea, and water accompanied the treats.

Each couple received a blue folder of materials, along with a branded pen. Jake struck up a conversation with one of the men seated beside us at the circular table, something about the pens. He was always able to connect easily with strangers. People were drawn to me too; we made a good team. I thumbed through the materials in the folder, started completing the questionnaire. Other couples filed in. I watched their faces. They looked hopeful too, but I could detect pain in their eyes. I tried to imagine their secret wounds. How many times had they tried? Who did they blame? When did they realize they needed help? Some of them looked tired, busy, flustered. Some seemed so young.

I admired the young ones. They were doing the smart thing looking into this now. I reflected on me and Jake. At least Jake had children with his first wife. That he was still willing to explore children with me at our age had been a plus. So here I was, over 50 and, until now, childless by choice. What right did I have to explore other options?

I was the one dumb enough to wait until the age of 50 to get married. I was the one too fearful to marry sooner. I had seen divorce. It was ugly. I was afraid. It wasn't that I lacked suitors. Men wanted to date 20- and 30-year-old me. But I'd had other goals. My divorced mother had encouraged me to explore the world before getting married. I was obedient. Marriage and a family weren't a priority for me then.

In the deepest places in my mind, where I didn't even allow my husband to enter, I thought about the men I had denied when I was fresh-faced and fertile. Back then, I took love and family-making for granted. Now here I was at 51 with 51-year-old eggs. All the things I had told myself over the years echoed in my head: "If you take care of your body, you are taking care of your eggs, you'll be fine." "It's in God's hands. If God wants you to have children, He will make a way." "When the right man comes along, it will happen."

I was sure I knew better than the doctors and my friends who had warned me about waiting too long.

And now here were four doctors lined up nicely before us. An older white man with a beard, a young, black woman whose bio said she was an HBCU graduate, a soft-spoken white woman, and a youngish man who looked like he could be Indian or Pakistani. Each one told their story and why they were drawn to this line of work. We were to imagine which one we'd like to work with.

Then they dug into the facts and figures of reproduction. A woman's eggs were with her from the moment of birth. They lost their viability as a woman crept into her 30s. Even if she was healthy as a tree, the age of the eggs mattered more. The more I heard, the more I realized that my chances to have a child this way weren't as bright as I had hoped. Maybe there was some way, some hidden technology we would discover in our one-on-one interview?

We selected the bright Black woman, Dr. Valeria Prescott. I figured she would understand my plight. Career would have come first for her too, I imagined. I didn't see a ring on her finger. Perhaps she hadn't married yet. I hoped we might bond in a different way than with the other doctors who presented themselves to us.

But as we toured the facility and then met with her in one of the offices, I felt my options slipping away, dripping out of my body like the blood from my monthly menses. Those annoying monthly periods had represented the precious fluid of my unfertilized children, wasted on tampons and maxi pads. Maybe I shouldn't have been so diligent, so obedient in my youth. Maybe I should have enjoyed wild, unprotected sex and had a baby out of wedlock. At least I would have had a baby.

At first I had been okay with not having children. It was when we started working on the family reunion on ancestry.com the year prior that I began to feel actual regret from my decision. Each branch on the ancestry.com family tree represented a family extension. When you wrote the relative's name on the branch, a new leaf emerged from the coupling like magic. I wrote my sister's name on a branch and my brother-in-law's. Then I wrote my nephew's name on the new branch.

My branch had been solo prior to Jake. After we got married, it felt so good to have a branch partner and to fill in the sprouts with his grown children and their mother. But there was no leaf for our combined progeny. Children represented continuing. They represented the expansion of the family history. I hadn't really thought about it like that before. I wanted the chance to expand the family tree.

In Dr. Prescott's office we learned of our dismal options: We could pay $10,000 or more to extract my old-ass eggs, but the prospects were poor, practically nil. My husband's eternal and ageless sperm were (of course) limitless. We could find the frozen eggs of a donor who looked like me to partner with his sperm. But there would be no DNA from my family tree. I had wasted my good genes because I refused to listen to my biological clock. I had rejected the hype.

Did we really want to spend $10,000 on a child that looked like me, but had half of my husband's genes and none of mine? Jake was quiet as always, not saying much. He seemed willing to go along with whatever I wanted. What I wanted was for him speak up more, provide some direction where I felt directionless.

Jake. Mr. Dependable. Stalwart and steadfast. Could he really have been that clueless about biology for people our age? It felt silly explaining to Dr. Prescott that with Jake's traveling demands on his job, we weren't having as much sex as older couples who wanted children should probably be having. Jake seemed completely fine with that, as if by divine intervention a child would be implanted into my womb like a middle-aged Virgin Mary. He didn't seem to appreciate that we needed to be putting in double and triple duty in the bedroom.

On my end, as a newlywed, I felt like the man should take the lead on these matters. I had waited so long for my husband and the societally condoned (and mother approved) marriage bed. But for some reason my husband chose TV, his family, washing the car, and everything else over getting it on with me. We enjoyed each other's company and spending time together, but Jake just didn't seem to have the same sense of urgency around the connection between having sex and getting pregnant.

When we left the clinic, we realized we didn't have time for lunch together.

"How do you feel?" I asked.

Jake shrugged and put the question back on me.

"I'm sorry my eggs are so old," I said.

"The important thing is that we have each other," he said. And that was so true. I had wanted a man who would want me regardless of children and one who would be willing to have them with me if we were able. I had found him.

We hugged, I smiled. I wish I had taken the day off. We'd talk later at home. Alone in my car, I held back my tears on the drive back to work. I felt like I had no right to cry. *Silly Rabbit, children are for women who try harder than you have.* There was still adoption or foster care, I told myself. We both wanted a family together. Jake was such as good father, and I loved his traditional values. If we could just talk things through and come to an understanding about our next steps, perhaps we could figure out what we wanted.

At the same time, I found myself frustrated with Jake. How could I put that into words? When we first got married, I tried not to stress too much that we hadn't transitioned into the sexual rhythm I thought most married couples would morph into as newlyweds. I wanted physical intimacy, not just to make a kid, but because I was attracted to my husband and I wanted to please him and be pleased.

We had limited our sexual activity once we became engaged in order to enjoy a more traditional wedding night, so that it might feel like the "first time." But after the wedding and a year into the marriage, we seemed to still be practicing the "let's hold off" method. I didn't even realize it was happening at first; I was so used to holding men at bay during my dating life to prevent pregnancy and because of my belief that sex was best in marriage.

But after a while our infrequent lovemaking began to feel abnormal. Was there a problem? I wondered. Did he not feel I was attractive or sexually desirable?

I broached the subject. Was he okay with "things?" Were we turning into the Ropers from that old '70s TV sitcom, *Three's Company*? Jake had said no. He loved me, he was attracted to me. We were fine.

Perhaps we should have had a capital-T Talk after the appointment. But Jake's job took him away that weekend, and soon, without us necessarily meaning for it to, the appointment had faded into the background of our busy lives. Jake had his job, I had mine. I continued to write and teach, buy groceries and take care of my ailing mother who lived two hours away. I was happy to have Jake. We did things together. We loved each other. Why rock the boat?

There was a part of me, deep and buried, that was glad we didn't talk about it. If we had talked, then I'd have had to stop and really think about what I'd lost in waiting all of those years. I'd have had to think about all of the men I had turned away, or forced into condoms. I'd have had to come to terms with all of the sexual exploration I had missed out on. So much time spent denying my sexual pleasure as young woman, waiting. I didn't even know I had a libido. It was is if my sex drive was hidden away, beneath the heirloom quilt I had socked away for safekeeping in my Lane cedar hope chest, passed down to me from my mother.

I had been a good girl, found a good man, and now this?

Maybe I should have let myself cry on the drive back to the office. Or when Jake and I found a moment to grieve together. I felt the sadness. I felt the loss. But I wasn't one to cry over spilt milk, or in this case, lost blood. I came from a family of strong Black women who cared more about thoughts than about feelings. Being vulnerable didn't come naturally to me. Why cry about something that had once been within my power to change? I was the one who had made those decisions, focused and clear-eyed.

And perhaps the biggest unnamed fear: If I allowed myself to feel the loss, would I lose myself, my sanity to a torrent of sobs and sorrow? I needed my Self and my sanity.

Maybe Jake and I should have set aside time to talk. Looking back, our marriage not only lacked a sexual rhythm, it lacked regular time to talk about what was really on our minds. Maybe we both thought we'd get to it eventually. We loved each other. I knew that. Maybe sharing our feelings would have bonded us in ways that never happened, maybe the course of our marriage would have played out differently.

Looking back, I can see how this disappointment led me to feel disappointment in other areas of my marriage. We both said we wanted children, but it didn't seem like Jake was as serious as I was about taking any steps toward helping us reach our goal. Instead, he retreated into silence, and this inability to verbalize his desires left an emotional and physical void within me that yearned to be filled. In the end, it was more than our new marriage could bear. We separated and have yet to find a way back to each other.

I did finally cry, though. The tears came to me as I read this story out loud during a writing workshop. There's some irony in the fact that I could reach in and pull out my guts with a room full of strangers in a way that I couldn't with my husband. My voice broke as I shared the snippet of what was to become a full-fledged essay. I guess the pain had been stored all this time, waiting for the right moment to emerge.

They were unexpected, cleansing tears. I wasn't at all embarrassed. I felt relieved.

Time

A.M. Ruggirello

Time ticks on
Grows long
Never stops
Never slows
A moment of peace
A breath of relief
Never shows
And then
Again
I'm all alone

Sometimes
The days react
To me
A backwards flow of time
Sometimes
I know the words
Hear the words
Trapped in my head
Melted into memories
Of sorrow
Loss
Despair
Circling the drain
Of what if?
Why me?

Why now?
Sometimes
All the time

The tick of time
Means the tears have dried
Once strong
Flowing
Endless streams
That leave behind
Every ache
Every pain
A piece of me
Day
By
Day
Where emptiness remains
Searching
For something
Anything
To fill the void
And make me whole

All that heals
Is time
But time
Sometimes
Takes,
Too

Prescription

A.M. Ruggirello

They say time heals all wounds
But what happens when time *becomes* the wound?

It passes over me
A trickle moving forward
Ever-present
An unavoidable reminder

that suffocates...smothers...strangles...
Any hope
Any prayer

Me

If time heals all wounds
But it's time I'm afflicted with
What prescription will you write for me, now?

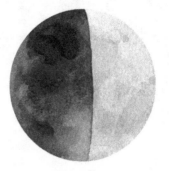

After the Worst Thing

Melissa Fast

I

I lay on my left side, staring out the window at the gray January afternoon. I watched cars in the distance stopping and starting at the intersections as if nothing had changed.

Lyle came in, shaking off his coat, leaning over the hospital bed to kiss me.

"What's going on?" he said.

"Dr. Isabelle was just here. I'm in labor, and one of the babies' sacs is leaking amniotic fluid. Nothing can be done for that baby, but there's a chance for the other one," I said, wanting my words to hold more than hope.

We both looked up to see a too-quiet ultrasound technician roll in his cart and come to the side of my bed. He untangled the cords and opened my hospital gown just enough to squirt goo onto my round, baby bump. He didn't offer to turn the monitor my way, and I didn't ask.

Not long after, Dr. Ruedrich, a high-risk obstetrician, came in. Pushing six-feet tall, he had several inches on Lyle, but both men shared a similar shiny, balding forehead.

Lyle cranked up my bed. I pulled up the crisp, white sheets and folded them under my arms. Dr. Ruedrich sat in a vinyl chair at the foot of my bed, and Lyle dragged an identical one from across the room. A small light on the wall behind me cast gray shadows across the floor of the darkened room. Light from the busy hallway just outside my room shot across Dr. Ruedrich's feet. My chart lay in his lap.

"Dr. Isabelle wanted me to come by and talk to you," he said. "I'm really sorry. I wish this conversation was easier. It's a hard one to have since you're only at 22-weeks."

Dr. Ruedrich explained that one baby's sac had ruptured. To limit the risk to me, I would need to deliver this baby within 24 to 48 hours, but it would not survive.

Since there were two separate placentas, there was a slight chance to save the other baby. Immediately following delivery of the first baby, Dr. Ruedrich could perform a heroic cerclage, which basically meant he would sew me shut. I would remain in the hospital on a bed tilted upside down to keep pressure off my cervix, letting gravity aid the huge amounts of medication keep contractions under control. The hope was that I would reach the 28-week marker. At this stage, nearly 100 percent of preterm babies survive with favorable outcomes. Still, infection risks to me would remain high.

I distanced myself from Dr. Ruedrich's explanations, hoping to find a better solution by asking just the right question.

"We perform a heroic cerclage trying to hold off delivery long enough for the other fetus to become viable," he said.

"What are the chances?" I asked.

"It's hard to say," he said.

"Like, is it 80/20, 50/50?"

"I wish I could say."

Why wouldn't he just answer the questions with certainty? In the moment, I thought he might be sidestepping opinions or even avoiding malpractice. I know now he had no good answers.

"How long do these procedures *typically* hold off labor?"

"Two weeks."

Why had we spent the last couple minutes dancing around words like heroic cerclage, favorable outcome, viable? Even today, very few babies born at 22 or 23 weeks survive, and babies born at 24 weeks, though viable, are still considered extremely premature.

Viable. A word that still sucks away my breath. To refuse medical intervention meant I chose to let both my children die. To try to save one baby, likely meant life-threatening breathing problems, cerebral palsy, blindness, deafness, and severe mental disabilities.

I sat in that hospital bed repeating, *this sucks, this sucks, this sucks,* wondering if it made me a monster to consider quality of life—not just for the twins, but the rest of our family.

I'd like to think my actions weren't impulsive, that they came only from wanting the best for the twins. I zoomed into autopilot. At the time, I would have said it was because I had to keep a clear head to make the best of an impossible situation. Yet, after nearly 20 years, I still go to the zone when I recall that evening. I won't dissect the memory—can't run the risk of finding a strand of hope that I missed. I also won't tell anyone that I still flip the channel on the TV if I come across a goddamn miracle story about premature babies.

"The other option is to induce labor and give birth to both babies knowing it is too soon for them to survive," Dr. Ruedrich said. "Even if you go this route, there's still a chance your cervix will naturally close after the first baby is born. If this happens, we could perform the cerclage and hope it holds."

Before the consultation, I had been in plan mode. I would be the perfect patient, no complaints. Bring it on. Invert the bed to relieve the pressure on my cervix. Tilt me completely upside down if you must. Pump the nauseating mag sulfate through the IV— let the room spin. I can handle it. I can even set aside the grief of losing one baby if it means keeping the other safely inside me.

"I know this is difficult. Because of the infection risks, we are asking you to make quick decisions. Do you have any more questions?" Dr. Ruedrich said.

Lyle remembers Dr. Ruedrich explaining the incredible risk for me, ranging from infection to death. I remember hearing the word "infection," but I only listened to what Dr. Ruedrich said about our babies.

"Melissa, did you hear Dr. Ruedrich? It's not just the twins. He says your life is in danger, too. What would I do without you? What would Russell do?"

The mention of Russell brought me back.

I wondered who would take our little boy to the zoo or make homemade bubble juice or stick toothpicks into his turkey and Swiss rollups. I was the one whose hair he twirled when we snuggled under the covers during nightly story time.

I would like to say that we took hours or even the rest of the night to make the decision. I block away the memory of doctors saying we could wait until morning to decide. Perhaps I should have given my babies one sleepless night before choosing to end their lives.

Instead, I lay in that hospital bed, digging my fingernails into the palms of my hands, cursing questions running through my head that I didn't know may haunt me forever: Why hadn't I called the doctor sooner? Was the early morning indigestion really labor? Would it have made a difference had I called an ambulance instead of driving myself to the hospital? I tell myself that hindsight is, of course, blindingly clear. I say that I made the best possible decision for everyone, but it doesn't stop me from wondering if I would have made a different choice had I given myself even an hour more to weigh the options.

"You're right. We need to induce labor," I said.

"I'll let Dr. Isabelle know," Dr. Ruedrich said. "I'm so sorry."

"I want an epidural. I don't want to feel anything."

"Of course," he said.

Lyle sat in the chair next to my bed. I lay on my left side, which I had always been told helped circulation to the babies. On this night, though, I'm not sure if my position was from habit, or hope.

When the nurse came in, she asked if she could sit next to me. Not once did she shift around or avert her eyes or pretend everything would be fine.

I wish I could remember her name; wish I knew where to find her to thank her for the kindness she shared.

"I want you to know what to expect tomorrow," she said.

Lyle reached over and took my hand.

The nurse explained I would be moved to a labor and delivery room the next morning where they would start a Pitocin drip, which would send me into full labor. The anesthesiologist would administer the epidural, and then Dr. Isabelle would deliver the twins.

"Do you have names picked out?"

Lyle and I looked at each other. He nodded, and I turned back to the nurse.

"Nolan Mitchell and Simone Renee," I said.

"It's hard to say how long Nolan and Simone will live," she said.

Lyle squeezed my hand.

"Their lungs aren't developed so they won't cry," she said.

"Will they be in pain?"

"No, babies born this early can't perceive pain," she said. "Have you thought about holding them?"

"Yes, I want to hold them."

Memory blurs here. The conversation with both Dr. Ruedrich and the nurse remain razor sharp. It had been so important to get all the facts of what was coming. However, in the moments after they left, neither Lyle nor I recall words between the two of us. I wish I could cling to a memory of Lyle sliding into bed next to me, the two of us talking and crying about what would never be. I suppose despair isn't that tidy. He was there. That I am sure, but sometimes words are so inadequate it doesn't do any good to voice them.

Yet, silence isn't always calm. Sometimes the quiet pounds and screams from the inside out. Things like: *This isn't fair. This sucks. I can't do this.*

The next morning, my nurse knocked as she opened the door and peeked in.

"You're still here," I said.

"I couldn't leave you," she said. "We're ready to move you to another room."

As the nurse helped me settle into the bed in the labor and delivery suite, I looked around at the floral print wallpaper and mauve walls of the birthing suite probably designed by decorators carrying around stacks of sample paint chips with names like Soft Hibiscus or Morning Paradise or Strawberry Fantasy.

The nurse started the Pitocin drip as a couple residents draped my legs. "The anesthesiologist will be in soon to give you the epidural, so you won't feel much."

Pitocin-induced labor forced my focus inward. Eyes closed. My head dropped to one side. Deep breaths replaced the rampant thought, "How am I going to get through this?"

From far away—even though he was right beside me—Lyle said, "Melissa. Melissa. Are you okay?"

His coffee breath mingled with the smell of starched hospital sheets and found its way into my next inhale.

"Okay. Hurts. Must breathe," or something similar. In all the years since, it never occurred to me as Lyle prepared to grieve his children in that room, he was just as worried about my well-being.

Labor progressed faster than the nurses and residents who bustled with sterile trays of medical instruments. I heard someone say there was no time for an epidural, and then someone else asked how close my doctor was, but Dr. Isabelle arrived just as the resident said, "She's completely dilated and effaced. We need to deliver."

Dr. Isabelle stepped between my draped legs held high in stirrups. There was no time for pleasantries. "Okay, push, Melissa.

You can do this," he said.

Lyle stood at my side and squeezed my hand. I cried and pushed and held my breath.

The baby slid between my legs into the doctor's hands. I crammed my tears back down. I was not finished.

Nolan was handed off to the nurse flanking the doctor.

An uneasy quiet filled the room.

"Call Ruedrich. I need a consult," Dr. Isabelle said.

Lyle and I didn't look at each other. We both knew Dr. Isabelle's words meant my cervix was closing. This was the slight chance that Dr. Ruedrich had discussed the night before. I had stuffed this fact down during contractions and had focused my thoughts on what I saw as my job. Get ready. Push now. Give birth.

In those seconds, not only did I reach out to grasp what Dr. Isabelle was saying, but new dreams surfaced. *Yes, saying goodbye to one baby will be hard, but it'll be okay. One baby is still here.*

Before the happiness could settle in, Dr. Isabelle said, "Wait... Never mind."

Minutes later, Dr. Isabelle passed Simone to the waiting nurse.

Shortly after 11:24 a.m., Lyle still at my side, the nurse placed the swaddled bundle in my arms. Through the hospital walls, echoes of "Congratulations!" and "He's so big!" seeped into my room. Both our babies were dwarfed in one soft, flannel square with blue and pink striped trim. I inhaled Johnson's Baby Wash and baby powder. I looked down at my tiny babies, skin purplish gray, chests pulsing, trying to breathe.

No comfort blanketed Lyle and me as it had when we had cooed over the twins' big brother in this same hospital five years earlier. How could I possibly say goodbye to children I had not cuddled or nursed or cupped my fingers around the gentle curve of their heads?

I told myself to breathe, and I wished for the end to arrive. Just. Let. Go.

I want to believe those words whispered over their heads don't make me a bad mother, but the memory won't fucking fade, and you may think time goes fast, but sometimes it just—stops. Even today, I wish I could rush this memory. Yet, it remains the only earthly moment I shared with my twins. I wasn't trying to capture a lifetime of mothering in that hospital room, but I knew that holding them would be the only thing I would ever do for them.

Lyle anchored my bed, stretching his arm across the pillows propped around my shoulders.

"I want to rock them," I said. "Help, me. I have to rock them."

Lyle called the nurse. She held Nolan and Simone as Lyle offered his arm and guided me across the room to the chair. "You don't have to do this, you know," he said.

"Yes, I do," I said.

We swayed forward and back, forward and back in the gliding rocker. I held each of their hands and counted five little fingers barely curled around the first joint of my index finger.

I would never clip these tiny fingernails.

*

Most days I can talk about the twins without spilling tears, but even now I hurry around two memories: Holding Nolan and Simone before they died and talking to Dr. Ruedrich after they passed.

That night of their delivery, Lyle and I heard a knock as Dr. Ruedrich peeked around the door and entered. Gone was the long white doctor's coat and scrubs, swapped for dress slacks, shirt, and tie. He pulled up a chair.

"I just want to say how sorry I am for your loss. I deal with high-risk cases every day. On really hard days I go home at night and cuddle up with my kids and try to find some gratitude. I hope you find some of that with your son," he said. "I've often wondered how I would deal with something like this. I just hope I could handle it with the grace and dignity that you and your husband have."

Holding them was horrible and hard and gut wrenching, but I

will never regret it. And I am forever grateful to Dr. Ruedrich for stopping by my room. I hang onto this gentle man's words as I try to shove aside the thought that perhaps I was just a selfish coward who refused the possibility to take care of a severely handicapped child.

As Dr. Ruedrich opened the door to leave, the happy comings and goings down the hall grew louder. Nurses tried to find another room for me, but there wasn't anything available on the same floor, or maybe there just wasn't a place for mothers with dead babies.

II

Other moms, the ones I met months after Nolan and Simone died, simply knew me as a mother of an only child. It was easier than explaining Russell was my *living* child. Too much information complicated play dates, so I let them believe I was just over-protective as I looked outside to make sure everything was okay.

In one memory, our kids play along the driveway in front of the house, far from the deserted road. The five-year-old boys hold fat chunks of sidewalk chalk, which they drop to the ground whenever they need to grab a swig of their Capri Sun drinks or handfuls of Goldfish Crackers. They wipe dusty pink and blue and green handprints over their shorts or across their sweaty foreheads before drawing the next big yellow dog or cat.

When I check again, Russell has finished the dog's body as his friend scoots across the pavement on his bottom, smudging the dog's stick-straight tail.

When I look out a few minutes later, Russell is lying down on the pavement, arms and legs splayed at odd angles as the other boy trace a white chalk outline of his body. I tell myself the chalky mess looks like a grotesque alien, but, still, I spray it away with the garden hose as soon as everyone left.

"They're fine, Melissa. You don't have to keep checking on them," the mother told me. "What's the worst thing that can happen?"

I kept my lips clamped and wished I could go back to a time when I mothered like this woman sipping her Diet Coke.

*

In the months after the twins' death, Russell and I snuggled down every night for bedtime stories. He couldn't voice how our life had changed, and I'm not sure I could have handled it had he been able.

Bedtime was the same as always: He picked out a stack of DK science and nature books and *The Chronicles of Narnia* and negotiated the amount of reading time. "Can we look at some tyrannosaurus pictures and then read *The Lion, The Witch and The Wardrobe?*" he said.

I feigned concern about the time and said, "Well, I guess, but you have to promise to go right to sleep, okay?"

"I promise, Mommy."

Our heads cuddled onto one pillow, his hand crept to the top of my head where he twirled my hair, one sleepy relic carried over from his nursing days as a baby when I held no doubt that I could keep him safe.

"I love you, Mommy."

"I love you, too, Russell.

I pulled in the sweet smell of the 2-in-1 blueberry shampoo and body wash he had picked out that promised tear-free fun.

"Will you lay with me for a little while? Just till I fall asleep?"

"Sure thing," I said.

His breath deepened as I lay there, feeling the heat radiate through his Elmo jammies.

I reached over to click off the light on the bedside table, covered with his daily finds: a rock with black and pink sparkly spots, three colorful pipe cleaners twisted into something spectacular, a rubber cockroach, and other little bits and pieces of things that he just couldn't let go of yet.

Infertility

Blaise Allen

At 40,

a deflowered

Amaryllis taunts me.

The Y shaped stalk

topped by dried

white papery pods,

a daily reminder.

The Fall

Blaise Allen

Hatless acorn, promise of hope,
marble of tree, nut of sustenance.
I roll you between my fingers,
shake the rattle of your heart.
Symbol of patience, laborious fruit,
fragrant rock. Placed on tongue,
I swallow your stony fetus,
Eucharist taken without faith.
Barren soil, nothing takes hold.
Deep bass of grief, not a single
note resonates. No lullabies.

To the ER Nurse

Kathryn Carson

I owe you an apology.

You had come in smiling.

I was the first patient on your rounds that night, just another woman flat on her back on a gurney, with a concerned-looking man sitting beside her. I was feeling alone despite my husband holding my hand; I had lost so much blood so quickly that I was afraid to stand up. He could hold my hand but he couldn't hold the blood in my body.

I'd never lost a pregnancy before. And neither had any other women of my family. Ever. My own mother, seeing my tears weeks later, would say, "I wish there was something I could say, but you're someplace I've never been."

My mother wasn't there that night. There was just me. And my husband. And you, the ER nurse.

You had come in smiling. A genuine smile, with warmth in it. Instantly, I could tell you cared, with your heart as well as your hands. I sank into your smile with gratitude. I needed that warmth in this lonely place.

You checked all of the extra parts that I'd acquired in that hospital bed...the tubes, the needles, the chart. "So what are we in for tonight?" you asked gently, as if volunteering to suffer together somehow.

"Miscarriage," I replied, just as your eyes caught the word on the page.

You paled. Your mouth shut as if pulled by impossible forces from inside. That smile disappeared from your eyes like a life

138

blown out. With shaking hands you put down my chart. You didn't quite run out of the room.

If I'd seen you again that night, I would've said I was sorry.

Sorry to blindside you. Sorry to hold my suffering up to you like a mirror. Sorry to so suddenly take you up on that offer, to suffer together. Sorry to have made you, a well-intentioned stranger, closer to me than family.

Syringes on the Breakfast Table

Alison Miller

I started birth control when I was sixteen. A variety of pills and implants ensured my steady periods and protected me against the fertilization that would doubtlessly occur without them. When my husband and I decided we were ready for kids, I tossed my last packet of pills into the trashcan with a flourish. It felt like transcendence.

Four weeks passed, and then four more. My period didn't come, and the drug store tests seemed devastatingly incompetent. *(How was it possible they kept reading negative when I still didn't have my period?)* I visited my OBGYN. She opened me up and her technicians poked at my veins. I wasn't ovulating, and she didn't know why. She said that my hormones matched that of a prepubescent girl or someone with anorexia. She ruled out early menopause and referred me to a fertility specialist.

During our first meeting, Dr. G drew a chart detailing all of the steps we might take to have a child. The last step on the list was adoption. He circled that word, and I felt grateful for his thoroughness and transparency. I became a patient of the Life Source Fertility Center in the same hospital where I was born.

Dr. G and I next met in what felt like the hospital's dungeon. He handed me shrink-wrapped socks and indicated the slab on which I was to recline as he pumped my fallopian tubes full of dye. I lay on my back while he directed my attention toward a screen showing slender veins of blue snaking through my abdomen like a phosphorescent sea creature. He pointed excitedly and said, "You have a blockage there. And there!" He pierced my blockages with an instrument that looked like it belonged in the hands of a demented dentist.

The puncturing of my blockages did not help, so we moved forward. We tackled forced ovulation with a pill that took two weeks to throw up its hands. Next up was injections. Several hundred dollars bought us small, highly corruptible vials of serum from England that my husband and I diligently stored on the top shelf of our refrigerator. We kept syringes on the breakfast table.

I visited Dr. G frequently, routinely discarding my pants in favor of a familiar stiff sheet, gazing at the covers of magazines devoted to news of Kate Middleton's first pregnancy. Dr. G measured my polyps on a boxy device, and, more often than not, asked me to return the next day.

Whenever his digital tape measure was satisfied with their size, Dr. G instructed my husband to administer the trigger shot, the one that would persuade my egg to drop. He warned us of the possibility of multiples. He talked about selective abortion.

When my mucus proved thin on top of it all, Dr. G suggested artificial insemination. Before work one morning, my husband drove his sperm to a medical building in a community structured around a shopping mall. A side effect of its insertion into me was a swollen belly, and for two weeks I studied my new bulge. I wore long tops over unbuttoned jeans and pretended I wasn't in the mood for wine. When my period was, for once, right on time, I bowed my head in the bathroom.

I conceived my daughter that May either as a result of artificial insemination or a heated telephone conversation in the dairy aisle of the grocery store. My husband was out of town and I was ovulating. I demanded that he come home, and he did.

When Ella was nine months old my doctor surprised me with the news that I was pregnant again. Three weeks later, at my first ultrasound, the technician asked bluntly, "Who told you, you were pregnant? Your uterus is empty." The fertilized egg had implanted in my fallopian tube, and I had to undergo surgery to remove what I'd thought was my child.

Women who have had an ectopic pregnancy are far more likely to have future ectopic pregnancies. My OBGYN advised me to wait several months before trying to get pregnant again. When my body was ready, we returned to Dr. G., and I conceived my son after one round of artificial insemination.

My kids are now seven and five. They are healthy and happy. They are best friends. Being a parent is every bit the beautiful, terrifying upheaval people say it is. Trying for children, struggling, being forced to consider a life much different than the one you planned is also a journey. Each day is long and full of heartbreaking uncertainty. I can't say I'm glad to have gone through it, but I'm grateful for its lessons. For every step, every moment, that led to my children.

Offering

Sarah Choi

Last year, on my son Bean's first birthday, my older brother's spirit connected with the family through my shaman sister. He was born before me and died at birth and remained a part of untold family history until I miscarried in my 30s. It wasn't until last year that we realized his soul was actively connected to the family, mostly to our mom. Korean culture in the 1970s, and the way my parents handled a crisis back then, meant no name, birth date, or acknowledgment of the baby. Yet, 40-something years later, on his only nephew's birthday, he was with us. Actually, all of my family ancestral spirits were present, asking "the one who keeps a temple" (aka my shaman sister) to formally invoke an invitation to this party they were very pleased about. If you came to Bean's birthday party (첫돌) last year, you would remember a small altar set up in the corner.

When we went home after the party, Bean was playing in front of us, as we sat in a circle around him. Then he turned his back to us to face a wall where there was clearly no one sitting, and started happily chasing something around, actively engaging and reacting, all the while laughing happily. It was so sudden, and my awareness of what was happening came slowly and quietly, but the second I realized he was playing with my brother's spirit my eyes went to meet my sister Seo's which told me she had just realized the same. I will never forget this moment.

Seo decided last year that she will honor our brother every year on October 31, because our mom thinks it may have been October when he was born. I named him 서진, a name that incorporates "Seo," part of the name my sister and I share as siblings, and adding "Jin," meaning the ultimate truth.

Seo is in Korea now, but remembering our brother this Halloween has been on my mind more than anything, certainly more than holiday festivities. I set up the altar like a toddler mom, offering milk instead of wine and fruit and snacks rather than a meal. Without thinking to, I caught myself saying out loud, "젖도 먹어보지 못하고 갔으니 오늘 우유라도 먹자." (Roughly, *Let's have some milk since you died without ever being breastfed by Mom.*) It wasn't until I heard my own voice saying those words that it occurred to me I'd never thought about what his short life must have been like.

I think what matters most is not the offering but that he is remembered.

Rainbow Baby

Karen Olshansky

Lonely, she cried for a baby sister or brother.
Her mother, distraught, depleted,
still stung from the infant born
blue and still, a boy
who would never play
with his big sister, never sing,
or run, or learn his letters,
took her daughter by the hand,
walked down the street
to the doctor, as if he could
just give the girl a shot of
penicillin to shrug
off her despondency.
No cure was offered, only,
"Have another child, Mrs. Rankin."
And so she did—
that was me,
born to console.

Emmanuel

Paula Michelle Gillison

My son was in my arms. The beautiful reality of my new normal enveloped me. I wouldn't eat the same way, sleep the same way, breathe the same way with him here. At that moment, I was mother, provider, saint; a Black woman about to do what Black women have always done: be strong. Even if it hurt or was uncomfortable.

The day I gave birth is etched in my mind like an old greeting card. The edges are frayed but there are so many feelings. The doctor came into the room and informed me that it was go-time. Four weeks early but I was confident. The next few hours were a blur. I remember the feeling of the needle in my back, the smell of flesh being cut and the pressure of organs being removed. I remember the silk of my mother's shirt pressed to my face. "It doesn't hurt, it's just uncomfortable."

I listened in desperate anticipation as the room fell silent. Then he cried. I could have melted into the floor. They weren't piercing cries, but they were striking. Melodic and enveloping. His cries grew louder as they brought my son close. His skin touched mine and his eyes squinted at the light. He stopped crying. He just looked at me intensely. It was almost like he knew words would pale. The moment lasted for 1,000 years, and then I fell asleep. I don't remember going back into the prep room. I don't remember the nurse coming in or my family consoling each other. I don't remember them asking me if I was ready to see him now.

When they brought him in, I was scared. I had never held a brand new human before. They put my son into my arms. His eyes were closed. His skin tasted so sweet against my lips. I spoke his name into his ear. Emmanuel Langston Gillison. I made promises to him and held him there for 1,000 years more. The nurse said I could. She said I could hold him as long as I needed to. So I held him until all the warmth from his skin melted into mine. Until I could no longer pretend to see his belly rise and fall. Until I had to ask my mother to take her cries into the hallway and the nurses to help me understand. Until I was ready to face the reality of my son's lifelessness.

I wanted my arms to be his coffin. I wouldn't eat the same way, sleep the same way, breathe the same way without him. At that moment, I was mother, provider, and saint; a Black woman about to do what Black women have always done: be strong. But I was also shattered and broken and undone.

I spent the next year reshaping my mind and my life. Religion could no longer answer for my faith. Faith could no longer mask my sorrow. I moved out of my house, quit my job. I ended some relationships, and I buried my son. I spent most days overwhelmed by the horror of what I was being asked to live with and most nights overcompensating for it. Drinking my sorrows away, being reckless with my body, trying to find anything that would fill the empty places of my soul. It wasn't until I faced the truth of my new normal that I was able to climb out of my despair and find peace.

I don't eat the same way, sleep the same way, or breathe the same way as before my son died.

When asked, I sometimes tell the truth; that I'm a mother without a child, that I hear him crying in my sleep, that I feel less than a woman and am afraid to try again. But other times, I lie.

Emmanuel is a healthy boy who loves 90s rap music and enjoys drawing dinosaurs. He speaks so clearly and reads far beyond his grade level. I never fight with him about eating veggies, and he tells me he loves me more than I deserve.

And I tell him I love him back every time.

It doesn't hurt as much anymore. But I've stopped trying to be mother, provider, and saint. I just am a Black woman doing what Black women have always done: be strong. And in being strong for Emmanuel, I found the strength to be strong for me.

Remembering You

Mary Helen Barker

Part 1

I never understood
the depth
of the word "tragic,"
until falling into its bottomless pit
was the only way
to be close to you again.

Part 2

Thinking of you
is as sweet
as holding a rose,
and as painful
as all of its thorns.
But for you
I will always open
my palms
and bleed.

Part 3

Of all the stars in the sky
in the constellation of my life,
you are one of the brightest.

A sun I will stare into
again and again,
even if it burns,
just to imagine your warmth.

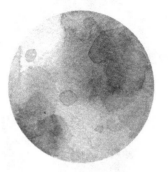

About the Contributors

Blaise Allen is the author of the poetry collection, *Happy Hour*, and has been the Director of Community Outreach at The Palm Beach Poetry Festival since 2006. Blaise bridges her passion of social welfare and the arts through community engagement and project management. Find her online at *www.Blaiseallenpoet.com*.

Dana Arlien is a playwright and fiction writer and was a semi-finalist in the Young Adult Novel Discovery Contest through Gotham Writers Workshop. She is a physician specializing in Child and Adolescent Psychiatry and has a strong interest in working with children and adolescents who are survivors of trauma and abuse. In her spare time, Dana enjoys trail running and cross-country skiing, and loves the adventure of traveling to new places. Having a strong appreciation for art, Dana says she writes because, "I can't paint." Dana's work has appeared in *Tahoe Blues, Short Lit on Life at the Lake*.

Mary Helen Barker is a student, Loss Mom, creative, and wife living in Northwest Arkansas. She is on a lifelong journey to learn how to navigate life in the wake of miscarriage. She began writing poetry after the traumatic loss of their first, Wilde, and it continued to be a meaningful outlet after the loss of their daughter, Marigold. You can follow along on her Instagram at *@Lady.MHB*.

Hanna Bartels received her BA in Creative Writing from Northwestern University and her MFA from Queens University of Charlotte. Her fiction has appeared or is forthcoming in *The Sun* and *Moon City Review* and her non-fiction has appeared in *The Manifest-Station*. She is at work on a novel about infertility and the fraught space between womanhood and motherhood. She lives in Minnesota with her husband and two dogs.

Allison Blevins received her MFA at Queens University of Charlotte. She is the author of the chapbooks *Susurration* (Blue Lyra Press, 2019), *Letters to Joan* (Lithic Press, 2019), and *A Season for Speaking* (Seven Kitchens Press, 2019), part of the Robin Becker series. She is the Editor-in-Chief of *Harbor Review* and the Poetry Editor at *Literary Mama*. Her work has appeared in such journals as *Mid-American Review, the minnesota review, Raleigh Review, Sinister Wisdom,* and *Josephine Quarterly*. She lives in Missouri with her wife and three children where she co-organizes the Downtown Poetry reading series. Find her at *www.allisonblevins.com*.

Kathryn Carson has a black belt in taekwondo. She also has MS and Hashimoto's and is an ocular melanoma survivor. Her work appears in print in Saint Leo University's *Sandhill Review*, as well as online at *Pyramid Magazine, The Mighty,* and her blog, *Sermons from My Desk,* at *katuvaggio.com*. She lives in Virginia with her best work: her kid and her husband.

Arden Cartrette is the writer and creator of the infertility and miscarriage blog, *Hello Warrior*. She chose to share her journey to motherhood with the world after a year and a half of feeling confused, disappointed, and alone. When Arden started opening up about her infertility, which later turned into recurrent pregnancy loss, she realized that there was an entire online community of women looking for support that they weren't getting in their daily lives. Through *Hello Warrior* her mission is to help women feel less alone while they go through infertility and miscarriage. Being an #InfertilityWarrior herself, she has found such a passion in raising awareness and helping others through the depths of loss.

Sarah Choi is a marketing strategist and community builder in Richmond, Virginia. Originally from Korea, Sarah says her spiritual life is a melting pot of sorts, incorporating buddhism, shintoism and Korean shamanism. When she is not roaming around the city planning Silent Reading Parties and hospitality events, you will find Sarah spending time with her son, Max, at her favorite Richmond destinations outside.

Melissa Fast is a nonfiction writer from Ohio, and she holds an MFA from Queens University of Charlotte. She currently works in marketing and public relations consulting. Her work was selected as one of the winners in the 2017 Carrie McCray Memorial Literary Awards from the South Carolina Writers Association, and she's also been published in *Minerva Rising, Bluestem Magazine,* and Brevity blog. Melissa is currently working on a book-length project, *The Worry Box: A Memoir of Finding and Letting Go.*

Paula Michelle Gillison is a poet and storyteller. With a passion for grief recovery and personal exploration, she expresses herself through parables and metaphors. Her work has been published and produced for the stage by The Billie Holiday Theater & "You Had Me At Black Storytellers." The author of poetry chapbooks *Under* and *Parables & The Gold Plated Things,* Paula also shares her art on her internationally recognized blog *For Lack Of Better Words.* She teaches creative writing for the organization *Life in 10 Minutes* and *The Writer's Den* poetry slam team while also being a supporter of all local arts. If there is ever downtime, she spends it with her large Southern family in Richmond, Virginia. All her passion is dedicated to the memory of her son, Emmanuel Langston Gillison.

Valley Haggard is the founder and director of *Life in 10 Minutes,* an online journal and press that provides a platform for writers of every experience level from all around the globe to write about their own lives...10 minutes at a time. The recipient of a 2014 Theresa Pollak Prize, a 2015 Style Weekly Women in the Arts Award and James River Writer's Emyl Jenkins Award for 2018, Valley has led local and international writing retreats and shares a writing center on Cary Street with Richmond Young Writers. Valley is the co-editor of *Nine Lives: A Life in 10 Minutes Anthology,* and the author of

The Halfway House for Writers and *Surrender Your Weapons: Writing to Heal.* She lives in Richmond, Virginia with her handsome husband, her brilliant son, two cats, a dog, and a bearded dragon named Monkey.

Angela Haigler burst into the writing world with her first job out of college as a television reporter. Preferring adventure over climbing the career ladder, Angela spent about ten years each in student affairs and library marketing. Along the way, she dipped a toe in her first love, Creative Writing, obtaining an MFA in Fiction from Queens University of Charlotte, one of the program's first graduates. Angela is a writer, writing instructor and coach, award-winning communications strategist, and the founder of Silverscrybe Communications & Consulting. She received a B.A. in Journalism from the University of South Carolina and an M.S. in the same from Iowa State University. Her work has been seen in Charlotte NC's African American lifestyle magazine *Pride* as its longtime book reviewer, *Beautiful Truths Digital Magazine, Change Seven Literary Magazine* and *Library Journal.* Angela is devoted to writing and cultivating the creativity in others.

R. Todd Henrichs is a poet and writer native to Florida and earned his BA in English at the University of Central Florida. He is currently working on a series of collected short stories that explore the subject of death, service, and sacrifice. He is an 8-year U.S. Navy veteran (Desert Shield/Desert Storm), facilitates a local writing group for the Florida Writers Association, and when not working, attempts to help his wife in wrangling their three cats (much to no avail). He has been published in *The Cypress Dome.*

Meredith Hill is a resident of Richmond, VA and has used writing to give voice to her life experiences since being encouraged to by her family at a young age. Her work tends to shine light on what it means to constantly redefine oneself through the seasons of life. After a long journey to pregnancy and through loss, she is now grateful to be growing into the role of motherhood, learning to write during brief pockets of time and encouraging her daughter to experience her life to the fullest and express herself freely, beginning now at the earliest age, and to one day, maybe write about it.

Jennifer Jurlando lives near Richmond, Virginia, where she is raising three sons with the help of an amazing husband and their dog, Skye. She was a contributor to the *Nine Lives* anthology and teaches Life in 10 Minutes classes for older adults. One day, she will paint a self-portrait. She will be carrying a wide, wooden bowl on her head, like the women in her Peace Corps village. The bowl will be swirling with the magic of words, stories, laughter, and tears that she has collected and held for the people who have shared their lives with her. Thistle's story and her legacy are there in the bowl, inviting you to tell your story, to give life to your beloved lost.

Linda Laino is an artist, writer, and teacher who has been making art in one form or another for over 40 years. Holding an MFA from Virginia Commonwealth University, she enjoys playing with words as much as form and color. Since 2012, she has resided in San Miguel de Allende, Mexico, where the surreal atmosphere and sensuous colors have wormed their way into her paintings. The last few years have found her making art at residencies around the world, most recently in Spain and France. Her poetry and essays have been published in anthologies and small presses such as, *The New Engagement, Sheila-Na-Gig Journal,* and *Sonder Midwest,* and in 2019 her poem, "Poem at Sixty," was nominated for a Pushcart Prize. In San Miguel, she is also known for her colorful and vibrant mandala murals. She is available for commissions. Her mandalas and other art work can be seen at *www.lindalaino.com.*

Lyndsey Lang graduated in 2007 with a degree in Creative Writing and English. She has a lifelong passion for writing, but it wasn't until her daughter was stillborn in 2016 that she started putting her writing onto a platform where people could read it. She created her blog, *After Evalyn*, detailing her and her family's journey after loss through various blog posts, quotes, poems, and songs. Many of her poems have been used by baby loss charities as a tool to demonstrate the grief parents face. In October 2019, she was awarded Author/Blogger of the Year at The Butterfly Awards.

Sarah Artley Luong is originally from Atlanta but has lived in the Richmond area for long enough to consider it home. Since 2004, she has taught at the Appomattox Regional Governor's School for the Arts and Technology in Petersburg, VA. She is deeply grateful for the opportunities she has each day to work with the wonderful students and teachers there. The struggle to carry a baby ruled her for years, but today she is gratefully a single mother of three hilarious and challenging children. These days she obsesses over potty training and Autism Spectrum Disorder and what to pack for lunches.

Katherine Meyersohn is a Licensed Clinical Social Worker and Founder & President of The Healing Arts Center of Richmond, specializing in a truly innovative, holistic approach to psychotherapy that integrates mind, body & spirit. Katherine has over 20 years of experience in holistic psychotherapy and wellness, incorporating a diverse array of complementary therapies including EMDR, Reiki, Yoga, GIM, MARI, Energy & Chakra Psychology, Plant-based Nutrition, and Past Life Regression Therapy, with more traditional psychotherapy, to foster clients' healing, personal growth, and optimal wellness. Katherine draws from a wealth of professional experience and knowledge in trauma, grief, and loss, as well as critical incident and crisis intervention work. She has been creating and leading Vinyasa & The Vineyard™ retreats, and Healing Spaces™ customized, experiential, holistic retreats, workshops, and wellness programs, including Practice Makes Peace™ self-care workshops, since 2011.

Alison Miller is the author of an unfinished memoir, a disorganized collection of letters, and a book that pretends to be about crystals. After a decade-long break from writing to focus on business and family, she created *Throats to the Sky*, a project that has evolved from sharing old journal entries to an outlet for new creative writing. Alison's poetry has been published in various literary magazines including *Hobart Pulp*, *Lynx Eye*, and *Illya's Honey*. The owner of sex-positive adult boutiques in Richmond, Virginia, she currently resides in San Diego. She offers sex writing workshops in Richmond and online. Find her work and info about upcoming events at *ThroatsToTheSky.com!*

Karen Olshansky is a retired psychotherapist who is thrilled to be writing poetry. Her poems have been published in *Tuck* magazine, in the anthology *Unsealing Our Secrets*, the *Literary Nest*, and in the anthology *Lingering in the Margins*. Karen lives in Richmond, Virginia, with her husband. She frequently visits San Francisco to bask in the energy and light of her grandchildren.

G.M. Palmer lives with his wife and daughters on a poodle farm in North Florida. His fourth daughter, Margaret, died at two months from SIDS. His work is online at *www.gmpalmer.com* and *@gm_palmer*.

Erin Pushman's other writing has appeared or is forthcoming in *The Gettysburg Review*, *Segue*, *Pangyrus*, *Confrontation*, *Mutha Magazine*, *1966: a Journal of Creative Nonfiction*, *Breastfeeding Today*, *Cold Mountain Review*, *Writing on the Edge*, *More New Monologues for Women by Women II* (Heinemann), *Boomtown* (Press 53), *WAVES* (ARAHO), and elsewhere. Her book, *Reading as a Writer: Ten Lessons* to *Elevate Your Reading and Writing Practice* is forthcoming in 2021. The recipient of a North Carolina Regional Artist Project Grant, she teaches at Limestone College. Erin blogs about her daughter's life as a critically ill child at *The Face of Bravery,* a WordPress blog and is currently working on a book about the maternal-fetal health crisis in America.

Christina Reed is a speech-language therapist by day and poet by night. She spends most days working with children to help increase their speech and language skills. Inspired by her fertility struggles and early pregnancy losses, Christina reaches an audience of women who are also grieving via her Instagram *@notpregnantpoetry.* Christina's poetry is raw, in your face, and crisp. Following the unexpected adoption of her son, Christina is writing a book of poetry entitled *Not Pregnant Poetry.* The collection is illustrated by her wife, and together they have mourned their losses by collaborating on this upcoming project. Christina is encouraged to continue writing in order to reach as many women as possible who are struggling to conceive, childless, or suffering loss. You can find her online at *notpregnantpoetry.com.*

Seema Reza is a poet and essayist and the author of the poetry collection *A Constellation of Half-Lives* (Write Bloody Publishing) and the memoir *When the World Breaks Open* (Red Hen Press). Based outside of Washington DC she is the CEO of Community Building Art Works, an arts organization that encourages the use of the arts as a tool for narration, self-care, and socialization among a military population struggling with emotional and physical injuries. In 2015 she was awarded the Col. John Gioia Patriot Award by USO of Metropolitan Washington-Baltimore for her work with service members. An alumnus of Goddard College and VONA, her writing has appeared online and in print in *Bellevue Literary Review, Green Mountain Review, The Washington Post, The LA Review, The Feminist Wire, HerKind, The Offing,* and *Entropy* among others.

Whitney Roberts Hill is a writer, editor, teacher, and seeker. Her work has appeared in *Streetlight Magazine, Life in 10 Minutes, Nanny Magazine, The Mighty, Jars of Wine, Germ Magazine,* and more. Whitney was named *The Woman Inc. Magazine's* Emerging Poet in 2019. She is a reviewer for the *American Book Review,* and a former editorial assistant at *Qu Literary Magazine.* Whitney has an MFA in Creative Writing from Queens University of Charlotte. She lives and works in Richmond, Virginia, with her husband and infant son.To learn more about Whitney, please visit *www.whitneyrobertshill.com.*

Ashley Ruggirello, who writes as "A.M. Ruggirello," is a young adult author, who lives in the world of fiction when reality sometimes becomes too hard to bear. Along with her husband, she has been dealing with infertility for the better of a decade. Since beginning their IVF journey, Ashley has used her words to put down and leave behind the feelings of the past with an optimism for the future. She is represented by Mandy Hubbard of Emerald City Literary Agency, and can be found online at *www.AMRuggirello.com.*

Carla Sameth's debut memoir, *One Day on the Gold Line,* was published July 2019. Her work on blended/unblended, queer, biracial and single parenting appears in a variety of literary journals and anthologies including: *The Rumpus, Collateral Journal, Anti-heroin Chic, The Nervous Breakdown,* Brevity blog, *Brain, Child, Brain Teen Magazine, Narratively, Longreads, Mutha Magazine, Full Grown People, Angels Flight Literary West, Tikkun, Entropy, Pasadena Weekly, Unlikely Stories Mark V,* and *La Bloga.* Carla's essay, "If This Is So, Why Am I?" was selected as a notable for the *2019 Best American Essays.* Carla is a member of the Pasadena Rose Poets, a 2019 Pride Poet with the City of West Hollywood, and was a PEN in The Community Teaching Artist. She teaches creative writing at the Los Angeles Writing Project, with Southern New Hampshire University, and to incarcerated youth. Carla has an MFA from Queens University of Charlotte (Latin America). She lives in Pasadena with her wife. Find her online at *www.carlasameth.com.*

Lisa Sharrock lives in the United Kingdom and founded *Still A Mama* in 2016 after her daughter Gracie was stillborn. *Still A Mama* has been created to break the silence of baby loss, honour all babies taken too soon, and to help loss mothers on their journey of building a new normal. It also provides an environment to open up about the tragedy that is parenthood after baby loss and enables loss parents the opportunity to be proud of their babies and the love they have brought to their lives. You can access *Still A Mama* via Instagram at *@still_a_mama* and Facebook, *Still A Mama*.

Acknowledgments

From Whitney:

I want to thank my own mother, first and foremost, for having the courage to try again so that I might exist, and for never hiding her lost babies from her living ones; it is because of you that I knew to honor and share my story.

Thank you to all the many friends and family members who shored me up through my grief; your presence sustained me, and transmuted my pain back into love.

Thank you to the Life in 10 Minutes organization, and especially to its founder, Valley Haggard, for creating a community of writers devoted to love and acceptance, and for giving us a platform to share these stories. May your mission shine on through this book.

The biggest thank you to Elizabeth Ferris, who approached me about this project, and spoke it into existence. Your compassion for others is a bright light in a sometimes dark world. Thank you for your many many many hours dedicated to this project, for being such a brilliant editing partner, the kindest of friends, and the best of teachers along the way.

Thank you to our donors for funding this project and spreading the word about it, to our cover artist, Sandra Kunz, to our creative director and graphic designer, the incredible Llewellyn Hensley, and the Life in 10 Minutes administrator, Nadia Bukach.

Thank you to the readers who will bear witness, and to the writers who have shared the tenderest of stories in these pages.

Lastly, thank you to my husband, Mark, for his abiding love, unending faith, and enduring support of my work in the world.

From Elizabeth:

Thank you to Valley for giving genesis and soul to Life in 10 Minutes Press, and to the many other people who have lent their time and great talents to our efforts: Llewellyn, Tim, Nadia, Becca, Hope, Henry, Claire, Camille, and Leah. We had two outrageously gifted interns who helped with stages of this book as well, Allison Tovey and Cana Clark. Thank you.

Thanks are due to my parents, family, and friends who have been first in line to buy our books, and to the wider Richmond writing community, who shows up for each other like no other; belonging to such a community is one of the great joys of calling myself a writer.

The thing about beginning to thank people is you realize how very many people there are to thank.

This book would not have happened without Whitney, for whose partnership on this project and in other matters I am forever grateful, and better, for. There would be no book either, of course, without the contributors, writers who have blown me away with the depth of their heart and wisdom and talent.

My final thanks is to Littleberry, who has supported me in this project in ways he knows and ways he couldn't. Thank you.

Colophon

Unspoken is typeset in Roslindale Text, a typeface designed by David Jonathan Ross. Named after a neighborhood in Boston, Massachusetts, the first style of Roslindale Text was released to Ross's *Font of the Month Club* in November 2017. It's an oldstyle typeface with "sharp, stubby serifs, bulbous terminals, and the occasional hint of diagonal stress." The result is clean and robust; helping create a sturdy, humanist vehicle for the stories contained here.

The book was designed by Llewellyn Hensley and Content-Aware Graphic Design in 2020.

Stories that are brave + true.

Homegrown in Richmond, Virginia, Life in 10 Minutes began with the mission to give passage to books we believe in. We seek to bring readers titles that are brave, beautiful, raw, heartfelt, and vital, and to nurture authors in their publishing journeys.

Learn more at *lifein10minutes.com/press.*

CPSIA information can be obtained
at www.ICGtesting.com
Printed in the USA
JSHW031739301220
10618JS00003B/166

9 781949 246049